COLLINS GEM

YEATS
ANTHOLOGY

HarperCollins*Publishers*

HarperCollins*Publishers*
P.O. Box, Glasgow G4 0NB

First published 1995

Reprint 10 9 8 7 6 5 4 3 2 1 0

ISBN 0 00 470880 6

Printed in Great Britain by
HarperCollins Manufacturing, Glasgow

CONTENTS

Poetry

Plays

Prose and Speeches

Quotations from:

W B YEATS

BY

A. NORMAN JEFFARES

Born in Dublin on 13 June 1865, William Butler
Yeats spent fourteen of his first sixteen years in
London, where his father, John Butler Yeats, had
brought his family in 1867. Called to the Bar, his
father had decided to become an artist. He was not
financially successful; he found it hard to decide a
painting was finished, and he charged too little for
his work. There was a feckless strain in him, and
income from the family land he had inherited
decreased steadily because of the Land War, a
decline in the economy and the drain of repaying
various mortgages. It would be cheaper to live in
Ireland and so John Butler Yeats brought his family
back to Dublin in 1881.

Like their mother, the Yeats children (Susan Mary [Lily] was born in Enniscrone in 1866, the others - they were Elizabeth Corbet [Lollie], Robert (d. 1873), John Butler (the painter, Jack) and Jane Grace (d. 1876) in London) had not liked living in London and had vastly enjoyed the time they spent in Sligo in the west of Ireland, where they stayed, often for long intervals, with their mother's family, the Pollexfens. They were, however, often terrified by their Pollexfen grandfather, and were more at ease with other relatives there, the Middletons. The Pollexfens owned mills and a shipping line which provided free transport for the family between Sligo and Liverpool.

Willie Yeats went to the Godolphin School in Hammersmith, then to the High School in Dublin from 1881 to 1883. After that he attended the Metropolitan School of Art in Dublin. At first the family lived at Howth, then a seaside village north of Dublin. Willie and his family travelled daily to Dublin, John Butler Yeats exerting a formative influence over his son, quoting his favourite poets and dramatists to him on the journey. Himself a considerable conversationalist, he encouraged his son to become a poet, impressed by his early work, and stressing his view that a gentleman should not be concerned with 'getting on'.

The young Yeats was in search of belief but had inherited some of his father's scepticism. His father, the son and grandson of Irish country rectors, had, he thought, made belief in orthodox Christianity impossible for him; he became a founder member of the Dublin Hermetic Society while still at school. Under the influence of John O'Leary (a former Fenian who had been sentenced to twenty years penal servitude and released after serving five on condition he went into exile, and who had returned to Dublin in 1885) he broke away from family tradition in his increasing interest in Irish poets who work in English and in translations of the Gaelic sagas; this complemented his awareness of myth and legend gained from peasants and others in Sligo. He formed friendships with Katherine Tynan, a poet and novelist, and with George Russell, who painted his mystic paintings and wrote under the name AE. He was beginning to get his poems published in Irish journals and to create a social life for himself in Dublin, meeting many Catholics in the process, when John Butler Yeats again moved his family to London (Willie was to stay at home until he was thirty) and they lived in Earl's Court, later at Bedford Park.

Now the poet had to make his way in a new milieu. He met William Morris; he was impressed by Madame Blavatsky and joined her Theosophical Lodge (but was soon asked to resign as he wanted proofs – his desire to believe was matched by his mind's sceptic, even mocking side). His long poem *The Wanderings of Oisin* was published in 1889; it was based upon his readings of Irish legends; it is romantic, escapist, mellifluous and at times melancholic. His first popular success was the lyric *The Lake Isle of Innisfree* of 1890. *The Celtic Twilight* (1893) gave its name to the kind of writing he was creating: dreamy, wistful, idealistic, defeated, evocative of moods. Irish legendary persons and places were an integral part of it. He began to form the idea of creating an awareness in Ireland of the country's mythology and history, almost lost and apparently being obliterated by British culture. In Sligo he had been deeply impressed by the local belief in the supernatural as well as folk memory of the pagan Gaelic tradition. It seemed to him that a synthesis of Ireland's pagan past could be blended with Christianity in a revived literature which would fuse both imaginatively.

He had to make a very meagre living by some journalism for American papers and by collecting and editing Irish material for London publishers. The family was very short of money and this depressed Mrs Yeats, who had suffered two strokes in 1887. The last of the family land in Ireland was sold in 1888, fetching disappointingly little when the mortgages were paid off. He met more authors and editors; among them were W. E. Henley, Oscar Wilde, John Todhunter, Florence Farr, York Powell and Edwin Ellis (with whom he edited Blake's poems in three volumes in 1893). He knew Lionel Johnson and Ernest Dowson, and, with Ernest Rhys, founded The Rhymers' Club which met in the 'Cheshire Cheese', a pub in Fleet Street.

A crucial moment in his life was his meeting Maud Gonne in 1889. He fell in love with her and offered to write *The Countess Cathleen* for her. She was a well-to-do, independent young woman who had become interested in Irish nationalism (urged to become Ireland's Joan of Arc by her secret lover, the French Boulangist Lucien Millevoye). Yeats had no money, and therefore, in the social conditions of the time, no prospect of marrying: he wondered what sort of wife Maud would make for a student, but nonetheless in 1891 he proposed to her, to be refused in terms she inevitably used whenever he proposed again. 'No Willie, the world will thank me for not marrying you. Let us continue to be good friends and go on writing me those lovely poems'. She inspired very many of them – throughout his life. In the 'nineties they tended to be defeatist, delicate and romantic, the most beautiful of them probably 'He wishes for the Cloths of Heaven'.

His poetry became more symbolist (*The Rose*, for instance, symbolised Intellectual or Spiritual Beauty, Ireland and Maud Gonne); it was esoteric in its blend of gaelic mythology and mysticism, reaching its extremes of dreamy beauty in the misty shadowy greyness of its adjectival moods in *The Wind Among the Reeds* (1899), a very *fin de siècle* volume, influenced by Yeats' membership of the *Hermetic Order of the Golden Dawn*, a magical society which he had joined in 1890, as well as his knowledge of Swedenborg, Boehme and Blake. *The Secret Rose* and *The Adoration of the Magi* were part of his plan to create a literary movement based upon Ireland's literary and spiritual past blended with his own mystic interests. He had formed Irish literary societies in London and Dublin, and he wrote many reviews and articles which were propaganda for the new writings of Irish authors.

While he pursued the nationalist aims he shared with Maud Gonne (who had achieved success in the relief of famine and in support of victims of evictions in the West of Ireland) to the extent of their both joining the Irish Republican Brotherhood, a secret revolutionary body, he also forced himself to undertake much public speaking in aid of the celebrations planned to mark the centenary of the Rising of 1798. He was also, however, coming under the influence of Lady Gregory. His first long summer visit – to be followed by one nearly every year – to her home, Coole Park, in Co Galway, led to her interest in the literary movement to which she contributed two fine volumes of translations, *Cuchulain of Muirthemne* (1902) and *Gods and Fighting Men* (1904). Even more significant was her support for his idea of creating an Irish Theatre. In turn this led to the establishment of the Abbey Theatre in Dublin in 1904, a project supported by a wealthy Englishwoman, Annie Horniman, a fellow member of the Order of the Golden Dawn, who paid for the conversion of a morgue into the theatre. Two years before this, Yeats' patriotic play *Cathleen Ni Houlihan* had had an explosive effect upon nationalist sentiment in Dublin.

About the turn of the century, Yeats' poetry changed – 'we all got down off our stilts', he remarked, and the first striking example of this is *Adam's Curse*. He shed the decorative, adjectival beauty of his early poetry – 'Now I may wither into truth', he wrote, and the spare but rhetorical poetry included more nouns and verbs, even permitting political topics in the forceful poems on the Lane controversy. Maud Gonne had married John McBride in 1903; the love poetry he wrote about her after that celebrated what was past; it was compelling nonetheless; he saw her now as a modern Helen of Troy: 'Why, what could she have done, being what she is?/Was there another Troy for her to burn?'

From 1904 to 1910 Yeats was deeply immersed in 'theatre business, management of men'. He fought for Synge's plays in the Abbey against hostile audiences, worked for plays with which he was often not in sympathy, and had to obtain funding for the Abbey when Mrs Horniman withdrew her support in 1911. His lecture tours in America had made him some money (the second one enabled him to repay loans Lady Gregory had made him so that he could give up journalism to concentrate on his own work); up to the turn of the century he had made about one hundred and fifty pounds a year (this was the amount of the Civil List pension he was granted in 1910). His work at the Abbey made him become more practical, often adopting a man of the world pose, a mask to cover his innate shyness.

He rented more rooms in Woburn Buildings (where he had first moved in order to pursue his first brief consummated love affair at the age of thirty with Mrs Shakespear in 1896). When his *Collected Poems* were published in eight sumptuous volumes in 1908 there were many who thought his poetic career was over. But *The Green Helmet* (1910) and, even more so, the powerful poems of *Responsibilities* (1914) began to show him moving in a new direction, praising the Renaissance rulers who had supported great art. His plays, notably *Four Plays for Dancers* (1921) were now designed for small, select audiences. He was moving to an appreciation of aristocratic society and was beginning to move in it in England, refusing a knighthood in 1915.

His world altered in 1916. Maud Gonne's husband was one of the leaders shot after the failure of the 1916 Rising (she had been separated from him since 1909). Yeats went to France where she was living at the time and proposed to her again, was refused in the usual terms, and a week later proposed to her daughter by Millevoye, Iseult. Iseult refused him in London and he married Georgie Hyde Lees on 20 October 1917. They had met in 1911, and shared an interest in mysticism and spiritualism.

Their marriage – he was fifty-two, she was twenty-six – led to a great reflowering of his poetry, largely through her automatic writing which led to

17

his book *A Vision* (1925; 1937). This gave him a great new self-confidence, and a system of thought that provided a scaffolding for his poems. These now combined the beauty of his early work with the realism of his middle period and had a new dynamic authority, new sets of symbols. These included the tower (relating to the medieval tower near Coole Park in Co Galway which he bought for £35 in 1917 and called Thoor, Ballylee). He and his wife restored it and spent summers there until 1929; the gyres of historical change and the phases of the moon which are both basic concepts in *A Vision*.

His dreams became reality. Married, he had a daughter and a son, so the Yeats line (in which he had become very interested when he began to write his autobiography in 1914) would continue. He returned to live in Dublin in 1922 after some years in Oxford. Eighty-three Merrion Square was the kind of Georgian house his father might have occupied had he been a successful painter. And he had his tower in Co Galway (it was near Coole Park and convenient for visiting Lady Gregory). He, the erstwhile revolutionary, was appointed a Senator of the Irish Free State in 1922. And he was awarded the Nobel Prize for Literature in 1923. The great poems of *The Tower* (1928) and *The Winding Stair*

(1933) confirmed his achievement and made him the leading modern poet. He wrote now of human love, historical change, the decay and destruction of civilisation , about people he had known, now dead, about his experiences in Ireland, a foretaste of the future elsewhere. He wrote, too, about the encroachments of old age, wondering to himself, as always, what might come after death.

In 1928 the Merrion Square house was sold and Yeats resigned from the Senate on grounds of ill health. (The family stayed at different times in Howth, Fitzwilliam Square, Dublin and Killiney before leasing Riversdale, an old farmhouse near Rathfarnham outside Dublin in 1932. In 1929 the family had spent its last holiday at Thoor, Ballylee).

As ever, Yeats was busy. He had chaired the Senate Committee on a new Irish coinage and written its admirable report; he had spoken effectively on matters relating to the arts and education. He had begun to discover what he thought was his intellectual ancestry in the eighteenth century; he read Swift (his play *The Words upon the Window-Pane* (1934) is a *tour de force*), Berkeley, Goldsmith and Burke (as well as innumerable detective stories). He undertook a last lecture tour in the United States and Canada; he made several successful radio broadcasts for the BBC. He edited the *Oxford Book of Modern Verse* (1892-1935) in 1936 and revised *A Vision* (1937).

His poetry gained in strength as he grew older. The vigour and outspokenness, the sheer technical virtuosity of *A Full Moon in March* (1935), *New Poems* (1938) and the posthumous *Last Poems and Two Plays* (1939) are full of sexual, political and personal directness. 'Myself must I remake' he wrote at the age of seventy-one.

The strength in his later poetry is the more impressive when seen against a pattern of increasing ill-health in his last fifteen years. Long years of overwork had taken their toll. He began to spend time in search of the sun; Sicily in 1924, Spain and Cannes in 1927, Rapallo in 1928 and 1929, Majorca in 1935 and 1936. Finally he went to France in 1938 and died there, writing some of *Last Poems and Two Plays* to within a few days of his death, which occurred at Roquebrune on 28 January 1939. His body was reinterred in Drumcliffe Churchyard, Sligo, in 1948.

THE LIFE AND TIMES OF WILLIAM BUTLER YEATS

1865	End of American Civil war. Ruskin, *Sesame and Lilies*. Swinburne, *Atalanta in Calydon*.	William Butler Yeats born in Dublin. Son of John Butler Yeats and his wife Susan (*née* Pollexfen).
1866	Prussia defeats Austria.	Yeats' elder sister Susan Mary (Lily) born at Enniscrone near Sligo.
1867	Second Reform Bill passed. Fenian Rising. Russia sells Alaska to the USA. Arnold, *On the Study of Celtic Literature*.	Family moves to 23 Fitzroy Road, Regents Park, London.
1868	Disraeli Premier for a year.	

1869		Elizabeth Corbet (Lollie) born in London. Church of Ireland disestablished.
1870	Franco-Prussian War. Third Republic declared in Paris. First Irish Land Act. D. G. Rossetti, *Poems*.	Robert Corbet born (d. 1873). Family holidays spent in Sligo.
1871		John Butler (Jack, the artist) born.
1872		Mrs Yeats and children in Sligo until autumn 1874.
1874	First Impressionist Exhibitions, Paris.	Family moves to 14 Edith Villas, West Kensington.
1875		June Grace born (d. 1876).
1876	Wagner completes *The Ring*.	Family moves to Woodstock Road, Bedford Park.
1877-81	National Land League founded in 1879.	WBY attends Godolphin School, Hammersmith.

1877-81		Holidays spent in Sligo with the exception of 1878 and 1879.
1880	Stanish O'Grady's *History of Ireland: the Heroic Period* completed. Parnell elected leader of the Irish party.	Income from lands in Co Kildare declines owing to Land War.
1881		Family moves back to Dublin, rent Balscadder Cottage, Howth.
1881-83		WBY attends the (Erasmus Smith) High School, Dublin.
1882	Phoenix Park murders of Lord Frederick Cavendish and T. H. Burke.	Family moves to Island View, Howth.
1884-86	Gaelic Athletic Assoc. founded.	WBY attends Metropolitan School of Art, Dublin.

1885	Ashbourne Land Purchase Act. Pater, *Marius the Epicurean*. Ruskin, *Praeterita*, (3 vols completed in 1888).	Family move to 10 Ashfield Terrace, Harold's Cross, Dublin. WBY attends first meeting of Dublin Hermetic Society. First poems in *Dublin University Review*. Meets Katharine Tynan, John O'Leary and Douglas Hyde.
1886	Gladstone's Home Rule Bill for Ireland defeated in Commons. Rossetti (d. 1882) *Collected Works*.	Begins reading Irish authors. *Mosada*.
1887	Victoria's Golden Jubilee. Parnell accused of complicity in the Phoenix Park murders in a letter published by *The Times*.	Family moves to 58 Eardley Crescent, Earls Court, London. Mrs Yeats has two strokes. WBY joins Theosophical Society. Meets William Morris.
1888	*The Times* letter exposed as a forgery. Moore, *Confessions of a Young Man*.	Family moves to 3 Blenheim Road, Bedford Park, where John Butler Yeats lives until 1902.

1888		Last of Yeats family land sold. WBY meets Lady Wilde, Oscar Wilde, Shaw, Henley and Rhys. *Fairy and Folk Tales of the Irish Peasantry*.
1889	Kodak manufactures camera using roll film. Eiffel Tower constructed.	*The Wanderings of Oisin*. Falls in love with Maud Gonne. Has met John Todhunter, John Nettleship and Edwin Ellis (with whom he begins editing Blake's *Poems*).
1890	Parnell cited in O'Shea divorce case. Re-elected to chairmanship of Irish party, but after Gladstone's remarks, alliance with Liberal party is denounced by Parnell, who in turn is rejected by the Irish party. Frazer, *The Golden Bough*.	'The Lake Isle of Innisfree'. Is asked to leave the Theosophical Society, founds the Rhymers' Club with Ernest Rhys and T. W. Rolleston, and is admitted into the Order of the Golden Dawn. Meets Florence Farr. Mildly affected in heart after collapse.

1891	Death of Parnell, buried in Glasnevin Cemetery, Dublin. Wilde, *The Picture of Dorian Gray*.	*Representative Irish Tales.* WBY friendly with Lionel Johnson and Ernest Dowson. Asks Maud Gonne to marry him (for the first time). *John Sherman and Dhoya.* Founds London Irish Literary Society with T. W. Rolleston (meets in January 1892).
1892	Hyde, 'On the Necessity for De-Anglicising the Irish People.' Nietzsche, *Thus Spake Zarathustra*	*Irish Fairy Tales.* *The Countess Cathleen and Various Legends and Lyrics.* Founds Irish National Literary Society in Dublin, with John O'Leary as President.
1893	Foundation of Gaelic League. Second Home Rule Bill passed in Commons, defeated in Lords. Hyde, *Love Songs of Connacht*.	*Works of William Blake* (3 vols, ed WBY and Edwin Ellis). Meets Lady Gregory in London. *The Poems of William Blake.* *The Celtic Twilight.*

1893	Wilde, *Salomé*. (English version 1894)	
1894	Irish Agricultural Organisation Society and Irish TUC founded. Moore, *Esther Waters*. Shaw, *Arms and the Man*. *The Yellow Book* (-1897).	First visit to Paris, stays with MacGregor Mathers. Proposes to Maud Gonne, with whom he sees Villiers de l'Isle Adam's *Axel*. *The Land of Heart's Desire* performed. Meets Mrs (Olivia) Shakespear. Experiments with symbols with his uncle, George Pollexfen, in Sligo. Visits Gore-Booths at Lissadell.
1895	Wilde, *The Importance of Being Earnest*. Wilde's trial and imprisonment for homosexual offences.	*Poems*. Shares rooms in the Temple with Arthur Symons (Oct 1895 – Oct 1896). *A Book of Irish Verse*.
1896	Connolly establishes Irish Socialist Republican Party. Marconi demonstrates wireless telegraphy.	Rents rooms in Woburn Building, London. Affair with Mrs Shakespear. Visits Aran Isles with Symons; they stay with Edward

1896	Becquerel discovers radio-activity. Nobel Prizes established.	Martyn at Tulisa Castle and visit Lady Gregory at Coole Park. Meets Synge in Paris when there to set up Order of Celtic Mysteries. Joins IRB (Irish Republican Brotherhood).
1897	Victoria's Diamond Jubilee. Bram Stoker, *Dracula*.	*The Secret Rose. The Tables of the Law: The Adoration of the Magi.* Disturbed by violence of Jubilee Riots in Dublin. First long summer visit to Coole Park. Begins *The Speckled Bird* (novel, published posthumously).
1898	Britain leases Hong Kong from China for 99 years. Britain conquers Sudan. Zola's open letter *J'accuse* defends Dreyfus. Wilde, *The Ballad of Reading Gaol.* Shaw, *Plays Pleasant and Unpleasant.*	Accompanies Maud Gonne on a lecture tour to Irish groups in England and Scotland, organising support for celebration of centenary of 1798 Rising. In Paris (April-May), in Sligo (September-November).

1898		Forms idea, with Lady Gregory and Martyn, of creating Irish theatre. 'Spiritual marriage' with Maud Gonne (first learns of her children to Millevoye).
1899	Boer War begins. Symons, *The Symbolist Movement in Literature*.	In Paris (February), proposed to Maud Gonne. *The Wind Among the Reeds*. *The Countess Cathleen* first performed in Dublin, first productions of Irish Literary Theatre (WBY a co-founder). At Coole until November.
1900	Protests against Victoria's visit to Ireland. Boxer Rising suppressed in China. Britain annexes Orange Free State and Transvaal. Freud, *The Interpretation of Dreams*.	Proposes to Maud Gonne in London; protests against Victoria's visit to Dublin. Leaves IRB, as does Maud Gonne. Forms new Order of Golden Dawn after rows with MacGregor Mathers and his envoy, Alistair Crowley.

1901	Death of Victoria, accession of Edward VII. (-1910).	Proposes marriage to Maud Gonne again. Resigns from Irish Literary Society. *Diarmid and Grania* (written disputatiously with George Moore) performed in Dublin. Meets Gordon Craig, sees Fay brothers acting, involved in experiments with psaltery with Florence Farr.
1902	Boer War ends. Lady Gregory, *Cuchulain of Muirthemne*. Conrad, *The Heart of Darkness*.	Lectures on the psaltery. Becomes President, Irish National Dramatic Society. *Cathleen Ni Houlihan* staged in Dublin, with Maud Gonne as Cathleen.
1903	Irish Land Act leads to tenants purchasing land. Ford founds car producing company. Wright brothers fly 852 feet at Kittyhawk, USA. Synge, *In the Shadow of the Glen*.	Maud Gonne marries John McBride. *Ideas of Good and Evil. In the Seven Woods*. Lecture tour in the USA arranged by John Quinn. Dun Emer Press (later Cuala Press) established in Dublin and run by WBY's sisters.

1903	Moore, *The Untilled Field*. Childers, *The Riddle of the Sands*.	*The King's Threshold* performed (April).
1904	Shaw, *John Bull's Other Island*. Synge, *Riders to the Sea*. Lady Gregory, *Gods and Fighting Men*. Royce produces his first car (combines with Rolls in 1906).	*Where There is Nothing*, performed, also *The Shadowy Waters*. Abbey Theatre opens in Dublin with WBY as producer/ manager. *On Baile's Strand* performed.
1905	Sinn Féin founded. Revolution in Russia after defeat by Japan. Trotsky forms the St Petersburg Soviet. Synge, *The Will of the Saints*. First cinema opens in USA.	National Theatre replaced by limited company. WBY co-director, with Lady Gregory and Synge, of Abbey Theatre. *Stories of Red Hanrahan*.
1906	Irish Nationalists support Liberals in House of Commons after election.	*Poems of Spenser*. *Poems 1899-1905*. *Deirdre* produced.

1906	Earthquake in San Francisco. Dreyfus re-admitted to French army.	
1907	France, Russia and Britain form Triple Alliance. In South Africa, Gandhi begins civil disobedience. Synge, *The Playboy of the Western World*. Joyce, *Chamber Music*. Picasso, *Les Demoiselles d'Avignon*. First Cubist exhibitions in Paris.	Crisis over Synge's *Playboy of the Western World*. Visits Italy with Lady Gregory and her son Robert. WBY's father goes to New York (dies there 1922). *Discoveries*.
1908	Asquith Liberal Prime Minister. Women's Freedom League established. First Model T Ford produced. Lady Gregory, *The Workhouse Ward*.	Start of affair with Mabel Dickinson. *Collected Works* (8 vols). Stays with Maud Gonne in Paris, 'mystical marriage' (June). Meets Ezra Pound. In Paris (Dec) working on *The Player Queen*.

1909	Lloyd George taxes high income in the 'People's Budget', which is rejected by the House of Lords. Suffragettes on hunger strike fed forcibly in prison. Bleriot flies the English Channel. Synge (d. 1909) *Poems and Translations.* Pound, *Personae.* Diaghilev brought Ballet Russe to Paris for first visit.	Lady Gregory ill. Quarrels with John Quinn. In dispute with Dublin Castle over Shaw's *Blanco Posnet.*
1910	Death of Edward VII. Accession of George V (-1936). Liberals bring in Bill to reduce powers of House of Lords, main issue in General Election.	*The Green Helmet and Other Poems.* Civil list pension of £150 p.a.. Disputes with Mrs Horniman over Abbey Theatre. George Pollexfen dies in Sligo.
1911	Parliament Act passed. Agadir crisis.	Miss Horniman withdraws financial support from Abbey Theatre

1911	Sun Yat Sen overthrows Manchu emperors in China. Amundsen reaches the South Pole. Moore, *Hail and Farewell* (vols 2 and 3 in 1912, 1914).	WBY goes to USA with Abbey company. Meets Georgie Hyde Lees.
1912	Asquith introduces Third Home Rule Bill. Scott reaches South Pole. *Titanic* sinks after hitting iceberg on maiden voyage.	Meets Rabindranath Tagore, writes Introduction for his poems. Stays with Maud Gonne in Normandy.
1913	Home Rule Bill rejected by House of Lords. Formation of Ulster Volunteer Force, Irish Citizen Army and Irish (National) Volunteers. Strike and lock-out in Dublin. Lawrence, *Sons and Lovers*. Proust, *A La Recherche du Temps Perdu* (first volume).	Experiments with automatic writing. Visits Mabel Beardsley in hospital. *Poems Written in Discouragement* dealing with Lane controversy. Stays at Stone College in Sussex with Ezra Pound acting as his secretary.

1914	Outbreak of First World War. Home Rule Act passed but suspended for duration of war. Panama Canal opened. Ezra Pound marries Mrs Shakespear's daughter, Dorothy. Joyce, *Dubliners*.	American lecture tour. Becomes interested in family history. *Responsibilities: Poems and a Play*. Finishes *Reveries over Childhood and Youth* (first volume of *Autobiography*).
1915	Sir Hugh Lane goes down with *Lusitania*, torpedoed by German submarine. Allied landing at Gallipoli fails (heavy casualties for Dublin Fusiliers). Einstein elaborates General Theory of Relativity.	Declines offer of knighthood.
1916	Vast casualties at battles of Verdun and Somme. Proclamation of Irish Republic. Easter Rising suppressed, Dublin bombarded.	Stays with Ezra Pound and his wife Dorothy (daughter of Mrs Shakespear) in winter.

1916	Leaders of Easter Rising shot after Courts Martial in Dublin. Compulsory military service in Britain. Joyce, *A Portrait of the Artist as a Young Man*. George Moore, *The Brook Kerith*. Jung, *Psychology of the Unconscious*.	*Reveries over Childhood and Youth*, first of *Plays for Dancers*, produced in Lady Cunard's drawing room. In Normandy in summer, proposes to Maud Gonne and then to her daughter, Iseult. Writes *Easter 1916*.
1917	USA enters war. London bombed by Zeppelins and later by Gotha bombers. Revolution in Russia. Bolsheviks withdraw from war by signing armistice with Germany Balfour's declaration of Jewish homeland in Palestine. Eliot, *Prufrock and Other Observations*. Valéry, *La Jeune Parque*.	Buys medieval castle at Ballylee, Co Galway for £35,which he calls Thoor Ballylee. Proposes to Iseult Gonne in Normandy; she refuses him in London. he marries Georgie Hyde Lees in London (20 October). She begins automatic writing. *The Wild Swans at Coole*.

1918	The Kaiser abdicates. Armistice ends war (11 November). Parliamentary Reform Act gives votes to men over 21, women over 30. Constance Gore-Booth (Countess Markiewicz) elected Sinn Féin M.P. (first woman M.P.). World wide influenza epidemic kills over 20 million people.	The Yeatses stay at Oxford, Glendalough, Sligo and Coole. They rent Maud Gonne's house, 73 St Stephen's Green, Dublin, until December. *Per Amica Silentia Lunae*.
1919	Fascist party founded in Italy. President Wilson establishes League of Nations. Civil War in Russia. First meeting of *Dail Eireann*, de Valera elected President. *Dail Eireann* declared illegal. Hitler forms National Socialist Workers Party. First transatlantic flights.	Anne Butler Yeats born in Dublin (26 February). Summer spent at Thoor, Ballylee. *The Player Queen* produced. Winter in Broad Street, Oxford. *Two Plays for Dancers*.

1920	Government of Ireland Act (Dec) partitions Ireland. Martial law declared as Sinn Féin rejects terms; fighting increases. 'Black and Tans' recruited, later 'Auxiliary' force set up to resist guerilla violence.	The Yeatses on lecture tour in America until May; last meetings with WBY's father in New York. Back in Ireland in the autumn.
1921	Anglo-Irish Treaty signed (Dec). Northern Ireland and Irish Free State established. Huxley, *Crome Yellow*. Strachey, *Queen Victoria*. Capek, *The Insect Play*. Pirandello, *Six Characters in Search of an Author*.	Michael Butler Yeats born (22 August) at Thame, near Oxford. WBY condemns British actions in Ireland at Oxford Union. *Michael Robartes and the Dancer*. *Four Plays for Dancers*.
1922	Treaty ratified by *Dail Eireann*, but rejected by Sinn Féin. Civil war in Ireland. Mussolini becomes Premier of Italy.	Buys Georgian house, 82 Merrion Square, Dublin. John Butler Yeats dies in New York. WBY awarded honorary degrees by University of Dublin and

1922	Stalin becomes Secretary of the Communist Party. Tutankhamun's tomb discovered. Joyce, *Ulysses*. Eliot, *The Waste Land*.	Queen's University, Belfast. Summer at Thoor, Ballylee. Becomes a Senator in the Irish Free State. *The Trembling of the Veil*. *Later Poems*. *The Player Queen*.
1923	Ottoman Empire ends with Mustapha Kemal Atatürk President of the Republic (-1938). Civil war ends in Russia with creation of USSR. O'Casey, *The Shadow of a Gunman*. Shaw, *Saint Joan*.	Awarded Nobel Prize for literature (in Stockholm for its award, December). *Plays and Controversies*. *The Gift of Haroun al Raschid*.
1924	First Labour government in Britain. Conservatives in power again (-1929). Death of Lenin. O'Casey, *Juno and the Paycock*.	*Essays*. *The Cat and the Moon*. Awarded honorary degree by University of Aberdeen. Final work on *A Vision*. Reading history and philosophy. Suffering high blood pressure. Visits Sicily (Nov) and Italian mainland.

1925	Treaty of Locarno. First surrealist exhibition in Paris. Hitler, *Mein Kampf*. Eisenstein, *The Battleship Potemkin*. Kafka, *The Trial*.	Visits Switzerland, Rome and Capri. Reading Berkeley and Burke. Speech against anti-divorce law in Senate. Spends May at Thoor, Ballylee.
1926	Riots over O'Casey's *The Plough and the Stars* at the Abbey Theatre. General strike in Britain. T. E. Lawrence, *Seven Pillars of Wisdom*.	*A Vision* (dated 1925). Chairs Senate Committee on coinage and writes its report.
1927	Trotsky expelled from the Communist Party by Stalin. First 'talkie' film. Lindberg first to fly the Atlantic solo. Kevin O'Higgins, Minister for Home Affairs in the Irish Free State, assassinated. Virginia Woolf, *To the Lighthouse*	Summer at Thoor, Ballylee. *October Blast*. Suffers congestion of lungs; ordered to take complete rest. Seeks sunshine at Algeciras, Seville (lung bleeding) and Cannes (there until February 1928).

1928   Kellogg Pact. Kuomintang under Chiang Kai Shek govern China. Joyce, *Anna Livia Plurabelle*. Lawrence, *Lady Chatterley's Lover*. Huxley, *Point Counter Point*.

O'Casey's *The Silver Tassie* refused by Abbey Theatre. *The Tower.* At Rapallo, April. Dublin house sold. At Thoor, Ballylee, June; in Howth, July. Last senate speech; resigns in July. Winter at Rapallo.

1929   Collapse of New York Stock Exchange. MacDonald Labour Prime Minister in Britain (-1931). Elizabeth Bowen, *The Last September*. O'Casey, *The Silver Tassie*. Graves, *Goodbye to All That*.

Winter at Rapallo. At Coole and last stay at Thoor, Ballylee in summer. In flat in Fitzwilliam Square, Dublin. *A Packet for Ezra Pound. The Winding Stair.* Serious attack of Malta fever at Rapallo. *Fighting the Waves,* (choreographed by Ninette de Valois, music by George Atheil).

1930	Gandhi leads passive resistance campaign in India. Wyndham Lewis, *The Apes of God*. AE (George Russell), *Enchantment*. Auden, *Poems*.	Portofino (till April). Visits Renvyle, Connemara (Gogarty's rebuilt house) in June, thence to Coole Park. *The Words Upon the Window Pane* produced at the Abbey Theatre. Visits Masefield, meets Virginia Woolf and Walter de la Mare. Winter in Dublin, in furnished house on Killiney Hill.
1931	Economic depression. Britain abandons gold standard. MacDonald forms 'National Government' (-1935). IRA banned in Irish Free State. AE (George Russell), *Vale and Other Poems*.	Awarded honorary degree by University of Oxford (May). Delivers most of MS for proposed *Edition de Luxe* of his works to Macmillan. Reorders finances of Cuala Press. Summer at Coole Park. First broadcast at BBC, Belfast.
1932	Eamon de Valera President of Ireland (becomes Prime Minister under the	

1932	new Constitution in 1937.) Roosevelt elected President of the USA (-1945). Stalin begins purges of Old Bolsheviks, army officers and intellectuals.	Winter and spring at Coole Park, where Lady Gregory was dying of cancer. Prime mover in foundation of Irish Academy of Letters. Leases Riversdale, Rathfarnham, Co Dublin. Last American lecture in the autumn. *Words for Music Perhaps and Other Poems.*
1933	Hitler appointed Chancellor of Germany. Concentration camps appear in Germany, which withdraws from the League of Nations. Roosevelt begins New Deal (-1939). Day Lewis, *The Magnetic Mountain.*	Meets de Valera. Interested in O'Duffy's Blueshirt movement for several months. *The Winding Stair and Other Poems. Collected Poems* (Nov).
1934	Nazi reign of terror in Germany. Austrian Chancellor Dolfuss murdered.	Stomach operation in London. Rapallo in June, Rome in the autumn. *Wheels and Butterflies.*

1934	Mao Tse Tung begins the Long March (-1935) across China. Beckett, *More Pricks than Kicks*. Pound, *The ABC of Reading*.	*Collected Plays*. *The King of the Great Clock Tower*. Friendships with Margaret Ruddock and Ethel Marrin begin.
1935	Italy invades Abyssinia. MacDonald succeeded by Baldwin (-1937). Penguin Books begin. George Russell (AE) dies. MacNiece, *Poems*.	Severe congestion of lungs. Stays with Dorothy Wellesley at Penns in the Rows, Sussex. Winters in Majorca. Shri Purohut Swami goes there to collaborate in the translation of the *Upanishads*. *Dramatis Personae*. *A Full Moon in March* (Nov).
1936	Death of George V. Accession of Edward VIII, who abdicates to marry Mrs Simpson. George VI succeeds his brother. Spanish Civil War begins.	Winter and spring in Majorca. Seriously ill; heart missing a beat. Nephritis. Margot Collis has an attack of madness. returns to Riversdale. Broadcasts for BBC on modern poetry. *Oxford Book of Modern Verse (1892 - 1935)*.

1936	Germany re-occupies the Rhineland. Jarrow workers' hunger march to London.	
1937	War between Japan and China. Picasso, *Guernica*.	Elected member of the Athenaeum. Three radio broadcasts for the BBC. *A Speech and Two Poems.* Begins friendship with Edith Shackleton Heald. *A Vision* (rev. ed.) (Oct). *Essays 1931 - 1936* (Dec).
1938	Germany annexes Austria. Munich Agreement seals fate of Czechoslovakia. Germany takes Czech Sudetenland. Beckett, *Murphy*.	*The Herne's Egg* (stage designs by Anne Yeats). In south of France (Jan – Mar). Stays in Sussex with Dorothy Wellesley and Edith Shackleton Heald. *New Poems* (May). Last appearance at Abbey Theatre, for performance of *Purgatory*. Maud Gonne's last meeting with WBY at Riversdale. Sussex (Sept), then to France.

1939	Germany invades rest of Czechoslovakia. Germany and USSR sign non-aggression pact. Germany invades Poland. On outbreak of Second World War, Ireland declares neutrality. Joyce, *Finnegan's Wake*.	Dies 28 January, buried at Roquebrune. *Last Poems and Two Plays. On the Boiler.*
1948		Body re-interred at Drumcliffe Churchyard, Sligo.

POETRY

THE STOLEN CHILD
1886

Where dips the rocky highland
Of Sleuth Wood in the lake,
There lies a leafy island
Where flapping herons wake
The drowsy water-rats;
There we've hid our faery vats,
Full of berries
And of reddest stolen cherries.
Come away, O human child!
To the waters and the wild
With a faery, hand in hand,
For the world's more full of weeping
*   than you can understand.*

Where the wave of moonlight glosses
The dim grey sands with light,
Far off by furthest Rosses
We foot it all the night,
Weaving olden dances,

Mingling hands and mingling glances
Till the moon has taken flight;
To and fro we leap
And chase the frothy bubbles,
While the world is full of troubles
And is anxious in its sleep.
Come away, O human child!
To the waters and the wild
With a faery, hand in hand,
For the world's more full of weeping
    than you can understand.

Where the wandering water gushes
From the hills above Glen-Car,
In pools among the rushes
That scarce could bathe a star,
We seek for slumbering trout
And whispering in their ears
Give them unquiet dreams;
Leaning softly out
From ferns that drop their tears
Over the young streams.
Come away, O human child!
To the waters and the wild
With a faery, hand in hand,
For the world's more full of weeping
    than you can understand.

Away with us he's going,
The solemn-eyed:
He'll hear no more the lowing
Of the calves on the warm hillside
Or the kettle on the hob
Sing peace into his breast,
Or see the brown mice bob
Round and round the oatmeal-chest.
For he comes, the human child,
To the waters and the wild
With a faery, hand in hand,
From a world more full of weeping than he can understand.

DOWN BY THE SALLEY GARDENS
1889

Down by the salley gardens my love and I did meet;
She passed the salley gardens with little snow-white feet.
She bid me take love easy, as the leaves grow on the tree;
But I, being young and foolish, with her would not agree.

In a field by the river my love and I did stand,
And on my leaning shoulder she laid her snow-white hand.
She bid me take life easy, as the grass grows on the the weirs;
But I was young and foolish, and now am full of tears.

CUCHULAIN'S FIGHT WITH THE SEA
1892

A man came slowly from the setting sun,
To Emer, raddling raiment in her dun,
And said, 'I am that swineherd whom you bid
Go watch the road between the wood and tide,
But now I have no need to watch it more.'

Then Emer cast her web upon the floor,
And raising arms all raddled with the dye,
Parted her lips with a loud sudden cry.
That swineherd stared upon her face and said,
'No man alive, no man among the dead,
Has won the gold his cars of battle bring.'

'But if you master comes home triumphing
Why must you blench and shake from foot to crown?'

Thereon he shook the more and cast him down
Upon the web-heaped floor, and cried his word;
'With him is one sweet-throated like a bird.'

'You dare me to my face,' and thereupon
She smote with raddled fist, and where her
son
Herded the cattle came with stumbling feet,
And cried with angry voice, 'It is not meet
To idle life away, a common herd.'

'I have long waited, mother, for that word:
But wherefore now?'
                              'There is a man to die;
You have the heaviest arm under the sky.'

'Whether under its daylight or its stars
My father stands amid his battle-cars.'

'But you have grown to be the taller man.'

'Yet somewhere under starlight or the sun
My father stands.'

                              'Aged, worn out with wars
On foot, on horseback or in battle-cars.'

'I only ask what way my journey lies,
For He who made you bitter made you wise.'

'The Red Branch camp in a great company

Between wood's rim and the horses of the sea.
Go there, and light a camp-fire at wood's rim;
But tell your name and lineage to him
Whose blade compels, and wait till they have found
Some feasting man that the same oath has bound.'

Among those feasting Cuchulain dwelt,
And his young sweetheart close beside him knelt,
Stared on the mournful wonder of his eyes,
Even as Spring upon the ancient skies,
And pondered on the glory of his days;
And all around the harp-string told his praise,
And Conchubar, the Red Branch king of kings,
With his own fingers touched the brazen strings.

At last Cuchulain spake,'Some man has made
His evening fire amid the leafy shade.
I have often heard him singing to and fro,
I have often heard the sweet sound of his bow.
Seek out what man he is.'

                                    One went and came.
'He bade me let all know he gives his name
At the sword-point, and waits till we have found
Some feasting man that the same oath has bound.'

Cuchulain cried, 'I am the only man

Of all this host so bound from childhood on.'
After short fighting in the leafy shade,
He spake to the young man, 'Is there no maid
Who loves you, no white arms to wrap you round,
Or do you long for the dim sleepy ground
That you have come and dared me to my face?'

'The dooms of men are in God's hidden place.'

'Your head a while seemed like a woman's head
That I loved once.'
                            Again the fighting sped,
But now the war-rage in Cuchulain woke,
And through that new blade's guard the old blade
    broke,
And pierced him.
                            'Speak before your breath is done.'

'Cuchulain I, mighty Cuchulain's son.'

'I put you from your pain. I can do no more.'

While day its burden on to evening bore,
With head bowed on his knees, Cuchulain stayed;
Then Conchubar sent that sweet-throated maid,
And she, to win him, his grey hair caressed;
In vain her arms, in vain her soft white breast.

Then Conchubar, the subtlest of all men,
Ranking his Druids round him ten by ten,
Spake thus: 'Cuchulain will dwell there and brood
For three days more in dreadful quietude,
And then arise, and raving slay us all.
Chaunt in his ear delusions magical,
That he may fight the horses of the sea.'
The Druids took them to their mystery,
And chaunted for three days.

                    Cuchulain stirred,
Stared on the horses of the sea, and heard
The cars of battle and his own name cried;
And fought with the invulnerable tide.

THE ROSE OF THE WORLD
1892

Who dreamed that beauty passes like a dream?
For these red lips, with all their mournful pride,
Mournful that no new wonder may betide,
Troy passed away in one high funeral gleam,
And Usna's children died.

We and the labouring world are passing by:
Amid men's souls, that waver and give place
Like the pale waters in their wintry race,
Under the passing stars, foam of the sky,
Lives on this lonely face.

Bow down, archangels, in your dim abode:
Before you were, or any hearts to beat,
Weary and kind one lingered by His seat;
He made the world to be a grassy road
Before her wandering feet.

A Faery Song
1893
Sung by the people of Faery over Diarmuid and Grania,
in their bridal sleep under a Cromlech.

We who are old, old and gay,
O so old!
Thousands of years, thousands of years,
If all were told:

Give to these children, new from the world,
Silence and love;
And the long dew-dropping hours of the night,
And the stars above:

Give to these children, new from the world,
Rest far from men.
Is anything better, anything better?

Tell us it then:
Us who are old, old and gay,
O so old!
Thousands of years, thousands of years,
If all were told.

THE LAKE ISLE OF INNISFREE
1893

I will arise and go now, and go to Innisfree,
And a small cabin build there, of clay and wattles made:
Nine bean rows will I have there, a hive for the honey-
  bee,
And live alone in the bee-loud glade.

And I shall have some peace there, for peace comes
  dropping slow,
Dropping from the veils of the morning to where the
  cricket sings;
There midnight's all a glimmer, and noon a purple
  glow,
And evening full of the linnet's wings.

I will arise and go now, for always night and day
I hear lake water lapping with low sounds by the shore;
While I stand on the roadway, or on the pavements
  grey,
I hear it in the deep heart's core.

WHO GOES WITH FERGUS?
1893

Who will drive with Fergus now,
And pierce the deep wood's woven shade,
And dance upon the level shore?
Young man, lift up your russet brow,
And lift your tender eyelids, maid,
And brood on hopes and fear no more.

And no more turn aside and brood
Upon love's bitter mystery;
For Fergus rules the brazen cars,
And rules the shadow of the wood,
And the white breast of the dim sea
And all dishevelled wandering stars.

Fergus — the man of action.

Aengus – the Celtic
God of Woods / Beauty ✓

THE SONG OF WANDERING AENGUS
1897

I went out to the hazel wood,
Because a fire was in my head,
And cut and peeled a hazel wand,
And hooked a berry to a thread;
And when white moths were on the wing,
And moth-like stars were flickering out,
I dropped a berry in a stream
And caught a little silver trout.

When I had laid it on the floor
I went to blow the fire aflame,
But something rustled on the floor,
And someone called me by my name:
It had become a glimmering girl
With apple blossom in her hair
Who called me by my name and ran
And faded through the brightening air.

Though I am old with wandering
Through hollow lands and hilly lands,
I will find out where she has gone,
And kiss her lips and take her hands;
And walk among long dappled grass,
And pluck till time and times are done
The silver apples of the moon,
The golden apples of the sun.

"unity of being sought"

Combination of Rosecrucea and Celtic thought

THE SECRET ROSE
1899

Far-off, most secret and inviolate Rose,
Enfold me in my hour of hours; where those
Who sought thee in the Holy Sepulchre,
Or in the wine-vat, dwell beyond the stir
And tumult of defeated dreams; and deep
Among pale eyelids, heavy with the sleep
Men have named beauty. Thy great leaves enfold
The ancient beards, the helms of ruby and gold
Of the rowned Magi; and the king whose eyes
Saw the Pierced Hands and Rood of elder rise
In Druid vapour and make the torches dim;
Till vain frenzy awoke and he died; and him
Who met Fand walking among flaming dew
By a grey shore where the wind never blew,
And lost the world and Emer for a kiss;
And him who drove the gods out of their liss,
And till a hundred morns had flowered red
Feasted, and wept the barrows of his dead;
And the proud dreaming king who flung the crown

And sorrow away, and calling bard and clown
Dwelt among wine-stained wanderers in deep woods;
And him who sold tillage, and house, and goods,
And sought through lands and islands numberless years,
Until he found, with laughter and with tears,
A woman of so shining loveliness
That men threshed corn at midnight by a tress,
A little stolen tress. I, too, await
The hour of thy great wind of love and hate.
When shall the stars be blown about the sky,
Like the sparks blown out of a smithy, and die?
Surely thine hour has come, thy great wind blows,
Far-off, most secret, and inviolate Rose?

HE WISHES FOR THE CLOTHS OF HEAVEN
1899

Had I the heavens' embroidered cloths,
Enwrought with golden and silver light,
The blue and the dim and the dark cloths
Of night and light and the half-light,
I would spread the cloths under your feet:
But I, being poor, have only my dreams;
I have spread my dreams under your feet;
Tread softly because you tread on my dreams.

THE OLD MEN ADMIRING THEMSELVES IN THE WATER
1903

I heard the old, old men say,
'Everything alters,
And one by one we drop away.'
They had hands like claws, and their knees
Were twisted like the old thorn-trees
By the waters.
I heard the old, old men say,
'All that's beautiful drifts away
Like the waters.'

NO SECOND TROY
1908

Why should I blame her that she filled my days
With misery, or that she would of late
Have taught to ignorant men most violent ways,
Or hurled the little streets upon the great,
Had they but courage equal to desire?
What could have made her peaceful with a mind
That nobleness made simple as a fire,
With beauty like a tightened bow, a kind
That is not natural in an age like this,
Being high and solitary and most stern?
Why, what could she have done, for being what she is?
Was there another Troy for her to burn?

ALL THINGS CAN TEMPT ME
1912

All things can tempt me from this craft of verse:
One time it was a woman's face, or worse –
The seeming needs of my fool-driven land;
Now nothing but comes readier to the hand
Than this accustomed toil. When I was young,
I had not given a penny for a song
Did not the poet sing it with such airs
That one believed he had a sword upstairs;
Yet would be now, could I but have my wish,
Colder and dumber and deafer than a fish.

To a Wealthy man who promised a
Second Subscription to the
Dublin Municipal Gallery
if it were proved the
People wanted Pictures
1913

You gave, but will not give again
Until enough of Paudeen's pence
By Biddy's halfpennies have lain
To be 'some sort of evidence',
Before you'll put your guineas down,
That things it were a pride to give
Are what the blind and ignorant town
Imagines best to make it thrive.
What cared Duke Ercole, that bid
His mummers to the market-place,
What th' onion-sellers thought or did
So that his Plautus set the pace
For the Italian comedies?
And Guidobaldo, when he made
That grammar school of courtesies

Where wit and beauty learned their trade
Upon Urbino's windy hill,
Had sent no runners to and fro
That he might learn the shepherds' will.
And when they drove out Cosimo,
Indifferent how the rancour ran,
He gave the hours they had set free
To Michelozzo's latest plan
For the San Marco Library,
Whence turbulent Italy should draw
Delight in Art whose end is peace,
In logic and in natural law
By sucking at the dugs of Greece.

Your open hand but shows our loss,
For he knew better how to live.
Let Paudeens play at pitch and toss,
Look up in the sun's eye and give
What the exultant heart calls good
That some new day may breed the best
Because you gave, not what they would,
But the right twigs for an eagle's nest!

ON THOSE WHO HATED 'THE PLAYBOY OF THE WESTERN WORLD', 1907
1914

Once, when midnight smote the air,
Eunuchs ran through Hell and met
On every crowded street to stare
Upon great Juan riding by:
Even like these to rail and sweat
Staring upon his sinewy thigh.

TO A CHILD DANCING IN THE WIND
1914

Dance there upon the shore;
What need have you to care
For wind or water's roar?
And tumble out your hair
That the salt drops have wet;
Being young you have not known
The fool's triumph, nor yet
Love lost as soon as won,
Nor the best labourer dead
And all the sheaves to bind.
What need have you to dread
The monstrous crying of wind?

THE COLD HEAVEN
1914

Suddenly I saw the cold and rook-delighting heaven
That seemed as though ice burned and was but the
    more ice,
And thereupon imagination and heart were driven
So wild that every casual thought of that and this
Vanished, and left but memories, that should be out of
    season
With the hot blood of youth, of love crossed long ago;
And I took all the blame out of all sense and reason,
Until I cried and trembled and rocked to and fro,
Riddled with light. Ah! when the ghost begins to
    quicken,
Confusion of the death-bed over, is it sent
Out naked on the roads, as the books say, and stricken
By the injustice of the skies for punishment?

THE MAGI
1914

Now as at all times I can see in the mind's eye,
In their stiff, painted clothes, the pale unsatisfied ones
Appear and disappear in the blue depth of the sky
With all their ancient faces like rain-beaten stones,
And all their helms of silver hovering side by side,
And all their eyes still fixed, hoping to find once more,
Being by Calvary's turbulence unsatisfied,
The uncontrollable mystery on the bestial floor.

THE WILD SWANS AT COOLE
1917

The trees are in their autumn beauty,
The woodland paths are dry,
Under the October twilight the water
Mirrors a still sky;
Upon the brimming water among the stones
Are nine-and-fifty swans.

The nineteenth autumn has come upon me
Since I first made my count;
I saw, before I had well finished,
All suddenly mount
And scatter wheeling in great broken rings
Upon their clamorous wings.

I have looked upon those brilliant creatures,
And now my heart is sore.
All's changed since I, hearing at twilight,
The first time on this shore,

The bell-beat of their wings above my head,
Trod with a lighter tread.

Unwearied still, lover by lover,
They paddle in the cold
Companionable streams or climb the air;
Their hearts have not grown old;
Passion or conquest, wander where they will,
Attend upon them still.

But now they drift on the still water,
Mysterious, beautiful;
Among what rushes will they build,
By what lake's edge or pool
Delight men's eyes when I awake some day
To find they have flown away?

IN MEMORY OF MAJOR ROBERT GREGORY
1919

I

Now that we're almost settled in our house
I'll name the friends that cannot sup with us
Beside a fire of turf in th' ancient tower,
And having talked to some late hour
Climb up the narrow winding stair to bed:
Discoverers of forgotten truth
Or mere companions of my youth,
All, all are in my thoughts to-night being dead.

II

Always we'd have the new friend meet the old
And we are hurt if either friend seem cold,
And there is salt to lengthen out the smart
In the affections of our heart,
And quarrels are blown up upon that head;
But not a friend that I would bring

This night can set us quarrelling,
For all that come into my mind are dead.

III

Lionel Johnson comes the first to mind,
That loved his learning better than mankind,
Though courteous to the worst; much falling he
Brooded upon sanctity
Till all his Greek and Latin learning seemed
A long blast upon the horn that brought
A little nearer to his thought
A measureless consummation that he dreamed.

IV

And that enquiring man John Synge comes next,
That dying chose the living world for text
And never could have rested in the tomb
But that, long travelling, he had come
Towards nightfall upon certain set apart
In a most desolate stony place,
Towards nightfall upon a race
Passionate and simple like his heart.

V

And then I think of old George Pollexfen,
In muscular youth well known to Mayo men
For horsemanship at meets or at racecourses,
That could have shown how pure-bred horses
And solid men, for all their passion, live
But as the outrageous stars incline
By opposition, square and trine;
Having grown sluggish and contemplative.

VI

They were my close companions many a year,
A portion of my mind and life, as it were,
And now their breathless faces seem to look
Out of some old picture-book;
I am accustomed to their lack of breath,
But not that my dear friend's dear son,
Our Sidney and our perfect man,
Could share in that discourtesy of death.

VII

For all things the delighted eye now sees
Were loved by him: the old storm-broken trees
That cast their shadows upon road and bridge;
The tower set on the stream's edge;
The ford where drinking cattle make a stir
Nightly, and startled by that sound
The water-hen must change her ground;
He might have been your heartiest welcomer.

VIII

When with the Galway foxhounds he would ride
From Castle Taylor to the Roxborough side
Or Esserkelly plain, few kept his pace;
At Mooneen he had leaped a place
So perilous that half the astonished meet
Had shut their eyes; and where was it
He rode a race without a bit?
And yet his mind outran the horses' feet.

IX

We dreamed that a great painter had been born
To cold Clare rock and Galway rock and thorn,
To that stern colour and that delicate line
That are our secret discipline
Wherein the gazing heart doubles her might.
Soldier, scholar, horseman, he,
And yet he had the intensity
To have published all to be a world's delight.

X

What other could so well have counselled us
In all lovely intricacies of a house
As he that practised or that understood
All work in metal or in wood,
In moulded plaster or in carven stone?
Soldier, scholar, horseman, he,
And all he did done perfectly
As though he had but that one trade alone.

XI

Some burn damp faggots, others may consume
The entire combustible world in one small room
As though dried straw, and if we turn about
The bare chimney is gone black out
Because the work had finished in that flare.
Soldier, scholar, horseman, he,
As 'twere all life's epitome.
What made us dream that he could comb grey hair?

XII

I had thought, seeing how bitter is that wind
That shakes the shutter, to have brought to mind
All those that manhood tried, or childhood loved
Or boyish intellect approved,
With some appropriate commentary on each;
Until imagination brought
A fitter welcome; but a thought
Of that late death took all my heart for speech.

*Airman – Major Robert Gregory
(son of Teddy Gregory)*

AN IRISH AIRMAN FORESEES HIS DEATH
1919

I know that I shall meet my fate
Somewhere among the clouds above;
Those that I fight I do not hate,
Those that I guard I do not love;
My country is Kiltartan Cross,
My countrymen Kiltartan's poor,
No likely end could bring them loss
Or leave them happier than before.
Nor law, nor duty bade me fight,
Nor public men, nor cheering crowds,
A lonely impulse of delight
Drove to this tumult in the clouds;
I balanced all, brought all to mind,
The years to come seemed waste of breath,
A waste of breath the years behind
In balance with this life, this death.

active

LINES WRITTEN IN DEJECTION
1919

When have I last looked on
The round green eyes and the long wavering bodies
Of the dark leopards of the moon?
All the wild witches, those most noble ladies,
For all their broom-sticks and their tears,
Their angry tears, are gone.
The holy centaurs of the hills are vanished;
I have nothing but the embittered sun;
Banished heroic mother moon and vanished,
And now that I have come to fifty years
I must endure the timid sun.

BROKEN DREAMS
1919

There is grey in your hair.
Young men no longer suddenly catch their breath
When you are passing;
But maybe some old gaffer mutters a blessing
Because it was your prayer
Recovered him upon the bed of death.
For your sole sake–that all heart's ache have known,
And given to others all heart's ache,
From meagre girlhood's putting on
Burdensome beauty–for your sole sake
Heaven has put away the stroke of her doom,
So great her portion in that peace you make
By merely walking in a room.

Your beauty can but leave among us
Vague memories, nothing but memories.
A young man when the old men are done talking
Will say to an old man, 'Tell me of that lady
The poet stubborn with his passion sang us
When age might well have chilled his blood.'

Vage memories, nothing but memories,
But in the grave all, all, shall be renewed.
The certainty that I shall see that lady
Leaning or standing or walking
In the first loveliness of womanhood,
And with the fervour of my youthful eyes,
Has set me muttering like a fool.

You are more beautiful than anyone,
And yet your body had a flaw:
Your small hands were not beautiful,
And I am afraid that you will run
And paddle to the wrist
In that mysterious, always brimming lake
Where those that have obeyed the holy law
Paddle and are perfect. Leave unchanged
The hands that I have kissed,
For old sake's sake.

The last stroke of midnight dies.
All day in the one chair
From dream to dream and rhyme to rhyme I have ranged
In rambling talk with an image of air:
Vague memories, nothing but memories.

IN MEMORY OF ALFRED POLLEXFEN
1919

Five-and-twenty years have gone
Since old William Pollexfen
Laid his strong bones down in death
By his wife Elizabeth
In the grey stone tomb he made.
And after twenty years they laid
In that tomb by him and her
His son George, the astrologer;
And Masons drove from miles away
To scatter the Acacia spray
Upon a melancholy man
Who had ended where his breath began.
Many a son and daughter lies
Far from the customary skies,
The Mall and Eades's grammar school,
In London or in Liverpool;
But where is laid the sailor John
That so many lands had known,
Quiet lands or unquiet seas

Where the Indians trade or Japanese?
He never found his rest ashore,
Moping for one voyage more.
Where have they laid the sailor John?
And yesterday the youngest son,
A humorous, unambitious man,
Was buried near the astrologer,
Yesterday in the tenth year
Since he who had been contented long,
A nobody in a great throng,
Decided he would journey home,
Now that his fiftieth year had come,
And 'Mr Alfred' be again
Upon the lips of common men
Who carried in their memory
His childhood and his family.
At all these death-beds women heard
A visionary white sea-bird
Lamenting that a man should die;
And with that cry I have raised my cry.

THE DOUBLE VISION OF MICHAEL ROBARTES
1919

I

On the grey rock of Cashel the mind's eye
Has called up the cold spirits that are born
When the old moon is vanished from the sky
And the new still hides her horn.

Under blank eyes and fingers never still
The particular is pounded till it is man.
When had I my own will?
O not since life began.

Constrained, arraigned, baffled, bent and unbent
By these wire-jointed jaws and limbs of wood,
Themselves obedient,
Knowing not evil and good;

Obedient to some hidden magical breath.
They do not even feel, so abstract are they,
So dead beyond our death,
Triumph that we obey.

II

On the grey rock of Cashel I suddenly saw
A Sphinx with woman breast and lion paw,
A Buddha, hand at rest,
Hand lifted up that blest;

And right between these two a girl at play
That, it may be, had danced her life away,
For now being dead it seemed
That she of dancing dreamed.

Although I saw it all in the mind's eye
There can be nothing solider till I die;
I saw by the moon's light
Now at its fifteenth night.

One lashed her tail; her eyes lit by the moon
Gazed upon all things known, all things unknown,
In triumph of intellect
With motionless head erect.

That other's moonlit eyeballs never moved,
Being fixed on all things loved, all things unloved,
Yet little peace he had,
For those that love are sad.

O little did they care who danced between,
And little she by whom her dance was seen
So she had outdanced thought.
Body perfection bought,

For what but eye and ear silence the mind
With the minute particulars of mankind?
Mind moved yet seemed to stop
As 'twere a spinning top.

In contemplation had these three so wrought
Upon a moment, and so stretched it out
That they, time overthrown,
Were dead yet flesh and bone.

III

I knew that I had seen, had seen at last
That girl my unremembering nights hold fast
Or else my dreams that fly
If I should rub an eye,

And yet in flying fling into my meat
A crazy juice that makes the pulses beat
As though I had been undone
By Homer's Paragon

Who never gave the burning town a thought;
To such a pitch of folly I am brought,
Being caught between the pull
Of the dark moon and the full,

The commonness of thought and images
That have the frenzy of our western seas.
Thereon I made my moan,
And after kissed a stone,

And after that arranged it in a song
Seeing that I, ignorant for so long,
Had been rewarded thus
In Cormac's ruined house.

MICHAEL ROBARTES AND THE DANCER
1920

He. Opinion is not worth a rush;
   In this altar-piece the knight,
   Who grips his long spear so to push
   That dragon through the fading light,
   Loved the lady; and it's plain
   The half-dead dragon was her thought,
   That every morning rose again
   And dug its claws and shrieked and fought.
   Could the impossible come to pass
   She would have time to turn her eyes,
   Her lover thought, upon the glass
   And on the instant would grow wise.

She. You mean they argued.

He.   Put it so;
   But bear in mind your lover's wage
   Is what your looking-glass can show,
   And that he will turn green with rage
   At all that is not pictured there.

95

She. May I not put myself to college?

He. Go pluck Athene by the hair;
    For what mere book can grant a knowledge
    With an impassioned gravity
    Appropriate to that beating breast,
    That vigorous thigh, that dreaming eye?
    And may the Devil take the rest.

She. And must no beautiful woman be
    Learned like a man?

He.   Paul Veronese
    And all his sacred company
    Imagined bodies all their days
    By the lagoon you love so much,
    For proud, soft, ceremonious proof
    That all must come to sight and touch;
    While Michael Angelo's Sistine roof,
    His 'Morning' and his 'Night' disclose
    How sinew that has been pulled tight,
    Or it may be loosened in repose,
    Can rule by supernatural right
    Yet be but sinew.

She.   I have heard said
    There is great danger in the body.

He. Did God in portioning wine and bread
    Give man His thought or His mere body?

She. My wretched dragon is perplexed.

He. I have principles to prove me right.
    It follows from this Latin text
    That blest souls are not composite,
    And that all beautiful women may
    Live in uncomposite blessedness,
    And lead us to the like – if they
    Will banish every thought, unless
    The lineaments that please their view
    When the long looking-glass is full,
    Even from the foot-sole think it too.

She. They say such different things at school.

UNDER SATURN
1920

Do not because this day I have grown saturnine
Imagine that lost love, inseparable from my thought
Because I have no other youth, can make me pine;
For how should I forget the wisdom that you brought,
The comfort that you made? Although my wits have gone
On a fantastic ride, my horses's flanks are spurred
By childish memories of an old cross Pollexfen,
And of a Middleton, whose name you never heard,
And of a red-haired Yeats whose looks, although he died
Before my time, seem like a vivid memory.
You heard that labouring man who had served my people.

    He said
Upon the open road, near to the Sligo quay –
No, no, not said, but cried it out – 'You have come again,
And surely after twenty years it was time to come.'
I am thinking of a child's vow sworn in vain
Never to leave that valley his fathers called their home.

EASTER 1916
1921

I have met them at close of day
Coming with vivid faces
From counter or desk among grey
Eighteenth-century houses.
I have passed with a nod of the head
Or polite meaningless words,
Or have lingered awhile and said
Polite meaningless words,
And thought before I had done
Of a mocking tale or a gibe
To please a companion
Around the fire at the club,
Being certain that they and I
But lived where motley is worn:
All changed, changed utterly:
A terrible beauty is born.

That woman's days were spent
In ignorant good-will,
Her nights in argument
Until her voice grew shrill.
What voice more sweet than hers
When, young and beautiful,
She rode to harriers?
This man had kept a school
And rode our winged horse;
This other his helper and friend
Was coming into his force;
He might have won fame in the end,
So sensitive his nature seemed,
So daring and sweet his thought.
This other man I had dreamed
A drunken, vainglorious lout.
He had done most bitter wrong
To some who are near my heart,
Yet I number him in the song;
He, too, has resigned his part
In the casual comedy;
He, too, has been changed in his turn,
Transformed utterly:
A terrible beauty is born.

Hearts with one purpose alone
Through summer and winter seem
Enchanted to a stone
To trouble the living stream.
The horse that comes from the road,
The rider, the birds that range
From cloud to tumbling cloud,
Minute by minute they change;
A shadow of cloud on the stream
Changes minute by minute;
A horse-hoof slides on the brim,
And a horse plashes within it;
The long-legged moor-hens dive,
And hens to moor-cocks call;
Minute by minute thay live;
The stone's in the midst of all.

Too long a sacrifice
Can make a stone of the heart.
O when may it suffice?
That is Heaven's part, our part
To murmur name upon name,
As a mother names her child
When sleep at last has come
On limbs that had run wild.

What is it but nightfall?
No, no, not night but death;
Was it needless death after all?
For England may keep faith
For all that is done and said.
We know their dream; enough
To know they dreamed and are dead;
And what if excess of love
Bewildered them until they died?
I write it out in a verse –
MacDonagh and MacBride
And Connolly and Pearse
Now and in time to be,
Wherever green is worn,
Are changed, changed utterly:
A terrible beauty is born.

THE SECOND COMING
1921

Turning and turning in the widening gyre
The falcon cannot hear the falconer;
Things fall apart; the centre cannot hold;
Mere anarchy is loosed upon the world,
The blood-dimmed tide is loosed, and everywhere
The ceremony of innocence is drowned;
The best lack all conviction, while the worst
Are full of passionate intensity.

Surely some revelation is at hand;
Surely the Second Coming is at hand.
The Second Coming! Hardly are those words out
When a vast image of *Spiritus Mundi*
Troubles my sight: somewhere in sands of the desert
A shape with lion body and the head of a man,
A gaze blank and pitiless as the sun,
Is moving its slow thighs, while all about it
Reel shadows of the indignant desert birds.

The darkness drops again; but now I know
That twenty centuries of stony sleep
Were vexed to nightmare by a rocking cradle,
And what rough beast, its hour come round at last,
Slouches towards Bethlehem to be born?

A MEDITATION IN TIME OF WAR
1921

For one throb of the artery,
While on that old grey stone I sat
Under the old wind-broken tree,
I knew that One is animate,
Mankind inanimate fantasy.

SAILING TO BYZANTIUM
1928

I

That is no country for old men. The young
In another's arms, birds in the trees
–Those dying generations–at their song,
The salmon-falls, the mackerel-crowded seas,
Fish, flesh, or fowl, commend all summer long
Whatever is begotten, born, and dies.
Caught in that sensual music all neglect
Monuments of unaging intellect.

II

An aged man is but a paltry thing,
A tattered coat upon a stick, unless
Soul clap its hands and sing, and louder sing
For every tatter in its mortal dress,
Nor is there singing school but studying
Monuments of its own significance;

And therefore I have sailed the seas and come
To the holy city of Byzantium.

III

O sages standing in God's holy fire
As in the gold mosaic of a wall,
Come from the holy fire, perne in a gyre,
And be the singing-masters of my soul.
Consume my heart away; sick with desire
And fastened to a dying animal
It knows not what it is; and gather me
Into the artifice of eternity.

IV

Once out of nature I shall never take
My bodily form from any natural thing,
But such a form as Grecian goldsmiths make
Of hammered gold and gold enamelling
To keep a drowsy Emperor awake;
Or set upon a golden bough to sing
To lords and ladies of Byzantium
Of what is past, or passing, or to come.

THE STARE'S NEST BY MY WINDOW
1928

The bees build in the crevices
Of loosening masonry, and there
The mother birds bring grubs and flies.
My wall is loosening; honey bees,
Come build in the empty house of the stare.

We are closed in, and the key is turned
On our uncertainty; somewhere
A man is killed, or a house burned,
Yet no clear fact to be discerned:
Come build in the empty house of the stare.

A barricade of stone or of wood;
Some fourteen days of civil war;
Last night they trundled down the road
That dead young soldier in his blood:
Come build in the empty house of the stare.

We had fed the heart on fantasies,
The heart's grown brutal from the fare;
More substance in our enmities
Than in our love; O honey-bees,
Come build in the empty house of the stare.

NINETEEN HUNDRED AND NINETEEN
1928

I

Many ingenious lovely things are gone
That seemed sheer miracle to the multitude,
Protected from the circle of the moon
That pitches common things about. There stood
Amid the ornamental bronze and stone
An ancient image made of olive wood –
And gone are Phidias' famous ivories
And all the golden grasshoppers and bees.

We too had many pretty toys when young:
A law indifferent to blame or praise,
To bribe or threat; habits that made old wrong
Melt down, as it were wax in the sun's rays;
Public opinion ripening for so long
We thought it would outlive all future days.
O what fine thought we had because we thought
That the worst rogues and rascals had died out.

All teeth were drawn, all ancient tricks unlearned,
And a great army but a showy thing;
What matter that no cannon had been turned
Into a ploughshare? Parliament and king
Thought that unless a little powder burned
The trumpeters might burst with trumpeting
And yet it lack all glory; and perchance
The guardsmen's drowsy chargers would not prance.

Now days are dragon-ridden, the nightmare
Rides upon sleep: a drunken soldiery
Can leave the mother, murdered at her door,
To crawl in her own blood, and go scot-free;
The night can sweat with terror as before
We pieced our thoughts into philosophy,
And planned to bring the world under a rule,
Who are but weasels fighting in a hole.

He who can read the signs nor sink unmanned
Into the half-deceit of some intoxicant
From shallow wits; who knows no work can stand,
Whether health, wealth or peace of mind were spent
On master-work of intellect or hand,
No honour leave its mighty monument,
Has but one comfort left: all triumph would
But break upon his ghostly solitude.

But is there any comfort to be found?
Man is in love and loves what vanishes,
What more is there to say? That country round
None dared admit, if such a thought were his,
Incendiary or bigot could be found
To burn that stump on the Acropolis,
Or break in bits the famous ivories
Or traffic in the grasshoppers or bees.

II

When Loie Fuller's Chinese dancers enwound
A shining web, a floating ribbon of cloth,
It seemed that a dragon of air
Had fallen among dancers, had whirled them round
Or hurried them off on its own furious path;
So the Platonic Year
Whirls out new right and wrong,
Whirls in the old instead;
All men are dancers and their tread
Goes to the barbarous clangour of a gong.

III

Some moralist or mythological poet
Compares the solitary soul to a swan;
I am satisfied with that,
Satisfied if a troubled mirror show it,
Before that brief gleam of its life be gone,
A image of its state;
The wings half spread for flight,
The breast thrust out in pride
Whether to play, or to ride
Those winds that clamour of approaching night.

A man in his own secret meditation
Is lost amid the labyrinth that he has made
In art or politics;
Some Platonist affirms that in the station
Where we should cast off body and trade
The ancient habit sticks,
And that if our works could
But vanish with our breath
That were a lucky death,
For triumph can but mar our solitude.

The swan has leaped into the desolate heaven:
That image can bring wildness, bring a rage
To end all things, to end
What my laborious life imagined, even

The half-imagined, the half-written page;
O but we dreamed to mend
Whatever mischief seemed
To afflict mankind, but now
That winds of winter blow
Learn that we were crack-pated when we dreamed.

IV

We, who seven years ago
Talked of honour and of truth,
Shriek with pleasure if we show
The weasel's twist, the weasel's tooth.

V

Come let us mock at the great
That had such burdens on the mind
And toiled so hard and late
To leave some monument behind,
Nor thought of the levelling wind.

Come let us mock at the wise;
With al those calendars whereon
They fixed old aching eyes,

They never saw how seasons run,
And now but gape at the sun.

Come let us mock at the good
That fancied goodness might be gay,
And sick of solitude
Might proclaim a holiday:
Wind shrieked – and where are they?

Mock mockers after that
That would not lift a hand maybe
To help the good, wise or great
To bar that foul storm out, for we
Traffic in mockery.

VI

Violence upon the roads: violence of horses;
Some few have handsome riders, are garlanded
On delicate sensitive ear or tossing mane,
But wearied running round and round in their courses
All break and vanish, and evil gathers head:
Herodias' daughters have returned again,
A sudden blast of dusty wind and after
Thunder of feet, tumult of images,
Their purpose in the labyrinth of the wind;
And should some crazy hand dare touch a daughter

All turn with amorous cries, or angry cries,
According to the wind, for all are blind.
But now wind drops, dust settles; thereupon
There lurches past, his great eyes without thought
Under the shadow of stupid straw-pale locks,
That insolent fiend Robert Artisson
To whom the love-lorn Lady Kyteler brought
Bronzed peacock feathers, red combs of her cocks.

TWO SONGS FROM A PLAY
1928

I

I saw a staring virgin stand
Where holy Dionysus died,
And tear the heart out of his side,
And lay the heart upon her hand
And bear that beating heart away;
And then did all the Muses sing
Of Magnus Annus at the spring,
As though God's death were but a play.

Another Troy must rise and set,
Another lineage feed the crow,
Another Argo's painted prow
Drive to flashier bauble yet.
The Roman Empire stood appalled:
It dropped the reins of peace and war
When that fierce virgin and her Star
Out of the fabulous darkness called.

II

In pity for man's darkening thought
He walked that room and issued thence
In Galilean turbulence;
The Babylonian starlight brought
A fabulous, formless darkness in;
Odour of blood when Christ was slain
Made all Platonic tolerance vain
And vain all Doric discipline.

Everything that man esteems
Endures a moment or a day.
Love's pleasure drives his love away,
The painter's brush consumes his dreams;
The herald's cry, the soldier's tread
Exhaust his glory and his might:
Whatever flames upon the night
Man's own resinous heart has fed.

LEDA AND THE SWAN
1928

A sudden blow: the great wings beating still
Above the staggering girl, her thighs caressed
By the dark webs, her nape caught in his bill,
He holds her helpless breast upon his breast.

How can those terrified vague fingers push
The feathered glory from her loosening thighs?
And how can body, laid in that white rush,
But feel the strange heart beating where it lies?

A shudder in the loins engenders there
The broken wall, the burning roof and tower
And Agamemnon dead.
                              Being so caught up,
So mastered by the brute blood of the air,
Did she put on his knowledge with his power
Before the indifferent beak could let her drop?

A MAN YOUNG AND OLD
1928

I

First Love

Though nurtured like the sailing moon
In beauty's murderous brood,
She walked awhile and blushed awhile
And on my pathway stood
Until I thought her body bore
A heart of flesh and blood.

But since I laid a hand thereon
And found a heart of stone
I have attempted many things
And not a thing is done,
For every hand is lunatic
That travels on the moon.

She smiled and that transfigured me
And left me but a lout,
Maundering here, and maundering there,
Emptier of thought
Than the heavenly circuit of its stars
When the moon sails out.

II

Human Dignity

Like the moon her kindness is,
If kindness I may call
What has no comprehension in't,
But is the same for all
As though my sorrow were a scene
Upon a painted wall.

So like bit of stone I lie
Under a broken tree
I could recover if I shrieked
My heart's agony
To passing bird, but I am dumb
From human dignity.

III

The Mermaid

A mermaid found a swimming lad,
Picked him for her own,
Pressed her body to his body,
Laughed; and plunging down
Forgot in cruel happiness
That even lovers drown.

IV

The Death of the Hare

I have pointed out the yelling pack,
The hare leap to the wood,
And when I pass a compliment
Rejoice as lover should
At the drooping of an eye,
At the mantling of the blood.

Then suddenly my heart is wrung
By her distracted air
And I remember wildness lost
And after, swept from there,
Am set down standing in the wood
At the death of the hare.

V

The Empty Cup

A crazy man that found a cup,
When all but dead of thirst,
Hardly dared to wet his mouth
Imagining, moon-accursed,
That another mouthful
And his beating heart would burst.
October last I found it too
But found it dry as bone,
And for that reason I crazed am
And my sleep is gone.

VI

His Memories

We should be hidden from their eyes,
Being but holy shows
And bodies broken like a thorn
Whereon the bleak north blows,
To think of buried Hector
And that none living knows.

The women take so little stock
In what I do or say
They'd sooner leave their cosseting
To hear a jackass bray;
My arms are like the twisted thorn
And yet their beauty lay;

The first of all the tribe lay there
And did such pleasure take–
She who would have brought great Hector down
And put all Troy to wreck–
That she cried into his ear,
'Strike me if I shriek.'

VII

The Friends of his Youth

Laughter not time destroyed my voice
And put that crack in it,
And when the moon's pot-bellied
I get a laughing fit,
For that old Madge comes down the lane,
A stone upon her breast,
And a cloak wrapped about the stone,
And she can get no rest
With singing hush and hush-a-bye;
She that has been wild

And barren as a breaking wave
Thinks that the stone's a child

And Peter that had great affairs
And was a pushing man
Shrieks, 'I am King of the Peacocks,'
And perches on a stone;
And then I laugh till tears run down
And the heart thumps at my side,
Remembering that her shriek was love
And that he shrieks from pride.

VIII

Summer and Spring

We sat under an old thorn-tree
And talked away the night,
Told all that had been said or done
Since first we saw the light
And when we talked of growing up
Knew that we'd halved a soul
And fell the one in t'other's arms
That we might make it whole;
Then Peter had a murdering look,

For it seemed that he and she
Had spoken of their childish days
Under that very tree.
O what a bursting out there was,
And what a blossoming,
When we had all the summer-time
And she had all the spring!

IX

The Secrets of the Old

I have old women's secrets now
That had those of the young;
Madge tells me what I dared not think
When my blood was strong,
And what had drowned a lover once
Sounds like an old song.

Though Margery is stricken dumb
If thrown in Madge's way,
We three make up a solitude;
For none alive today
Can know the stories that we know
Or say the things we say:

How such a man pleased women most
Of all that are gone,
How such a pair loved many years
And such a pair but one,
Stories of the bed of straw
Or the bed of down.

X

His Wildness

O bid me mount and sail up there
Amid the cloudy wrack,
For Peg and Meg and Paris' love
That had so straight a back,
Are gone away, and some that stay
Have changed their silk for sack.

Were I but there and none to hear
I'd have a peacock cry,
For that is natural to a man
That lives in memory,
Being all alone I'd nurse a stone
And sing it lullaby.

XI

From 'Oedipus at Colonus'

Endure what life God gives and ask no longer span;
Cease to remember the delights of youth, travel-
    wearied aged man;
Delight becomes death-longing if all longing else be
    vain.

Even from that delight memory treasures so,
Death, despair, division of families, all entanglements
    of mankind grow,
As that old wandering beggar and these God-hated
    children know.

In the long echoing street the laughing dancers throng,
The bride is carried to the bridegroom's chamber
    through torchlight and tumultuous song;
I celebrate the silent kiss that ends short life or long.

Never to have lived is best, the ancient writers say;
Never to have drawn the breath of life, never to have
    looked into the eye of day;
The second best's a gay goodnight and quickly turn
    away.

A DIALOGUE OF SELF AND SOUL
1933

I

My Soul. I summon to the winding ancient stair;
   Set all your mind upon the steep ascent,
   Upon the broken crumbling battlement,
   Upon the breathless starlit air,
   Upon the star that marks the hidden pole;
   Fix every wandering thought upon
   That quarter where all thought is done:
   Who can distinguish darkness from the soul?

My Self. The consecrated blade upon my knees
   Is Sato's ancient blade, still as it was,
   Still razor-keen, still like a looking glass
   Unspotted by the centuries;
   That flowering, silken, old embroidery, torn
   From some court-lady's dress and round
   The wooden scabbard bound and wound,
   Can, tattered, still protect, faded adorn.

My Soul. Why should the imagination of a man
    Long past his prime remember things that are
    Emblematical of love and war?
    Think of ancestral night that can,
    If but imagination scorn the earth
    And intellect its wandering
    To this and that and t'other thing,
    Deliver from the crime of death and birth.

My Self. Montashigi, third of his family, fashioned it
    Five hundred years ago, about it lie
    Flowers from I know not what embroidery–
    Heart's purple–and all these I set
    For emblems of the day against the tower
    Emblematical of the night,
    And claim as by a soldier's right
    A charter to commit the crime once more.

My Soul. Such fullness in that quarter overflows
    And falls into the basin of the mind
    That man is stricken deaf and dumb and blind,
    For intellect no longer knows
    Is from the *Ought*, or *Knower* from the *Known*–
    That is to say, ascends to Heaven;
    Only the dead can be forgiven;
    But when I think of that my tongue's a stone.

II

My Self. A living man is blind and drinks his drop.
What matter if the ditches are impure?
What matter if I live it all once more?
Endure that toil of growing up;
The ignominy of boyhood; the distress
Of boyhood changing into man;
The unfinished man and his pain
Brought face to face with his own clumsiness;

The finished man among his enemies?–
How in the name of Heaven can he escape
That defiling and disfigured shape
The mirror of malicious eyes
Casts upon his eyes until at last
He thinks that shape must be his shape?
And what's the good of an escape
If honour find him in the wintry blast?

I am content to live it all again
And yet again, if it be life to pitch
Into the frog-spawn of a blind man's ditch,
A blind man battering blind men;
Or into that most fecund ditch of all,
The folly that man does
Or must suffer, if he woos
A proud woman not kindred of his soul.

I am content to follow to its source
Every event in action or in thought;
Measure the lot; forgive myself the lot!
When such as I cast out remorse
So great a sweetness flows into the breast
We must laugh and we must sing,
We are blest by everythying,
Everything we look upon is blest.

THE NINETEENTH CENTURY AND AFTER
1933

Though the great song return no more
There's keen delight in what we have:
The rattle of pebbles on the shore
Under the receding wave.

THREE MOVEMENTS
1933

Shakespearean fish swam the sea, far away from land;
Romantic fish swam in nets coming to the hand;
Where are all those fish that lie gasping on the strand?

THE CRAZED MOON
1933

Crazed through much child-bearing
The moon is staggering in the sky;
Moon-struck by the despairing
Glances of her wandering eye
We grope, and grope in vain,
For children born of her pain.

Children dazed or dead!
When she in all her virginal pride
First trod on the mountain's head
What stir ran through the countryside
Where every foot obeyed her glance!
What manhood led the dance!

Fly-catchers of the moon,
Our hands are blenched, our fingers seem
But slender needles of bone;
Blenched by that malicious dream
They are spread wide that each
May rend what comes in reach.

COOLE PARK, 1929
1933

I meditate upon a swallow's flight,
Upon an aged woman and her house,
A sycamore and lime-tree lost in night
Although that western cloud is luminous,
Great works constructed there in nature's spite
For scholars and for poets after us,
Thoughts long knitted into a single thought,
A dance-like glory that those walls begot.

There Hyde before he had been beaten into prose
That noble blade the Muses buckled on,
There one that ruffled in a manly pose
For all his timid heart, there that slow man,
That meditative man, John Synge, and those
Impetuous men, Shawe-Taylor and Hugh Lane,
Found pride established in humility,
A scene well set and excellent company.

They came like swallows and like swallows went,
And yet a woman's powerful character
Could keep a swallow to its first intent;
And half a dozen in formation there,
That seemed to whirl upon a compass point,
Found certainty upon the dreaming air,
The intellectual sweetness of those lines
That cut through time or cross it withershins.

Here, traveller, scholar, poet, take your stand
When all those rooms and passages are gone,
When nettles wave upon a shapeless mound
And saplings root among the broken stone,
And dedicate – eyes bent upon the ground,
Back turned upon the brightness of the sun
And all the sensuality of the shade –
A moment's memory of that laurelled head.

COOLE PARK AND BALLYLEE, 1931
1933

Under my window-ledge the waters race,
Otters below and moor-hens on the top,
Run for a mile undimmed in Heaven's face
Then darkening through 'dark' Raftery's 'cellar' drop,
Run underground, rise in a rocky place
In Coole demesne, and there to finish up
Spread to a lake and drop into a hole.
What's water but the generated soul?

Upon the border of that lake's a wood
Now all dry sticks under a wintry sun,
And in a copse of beeches there I stood,
For Nature's pulled her tragic buskin on
And all the rant's a mirror of my mood:
At sudden thunder of the mounting swan
I turned about and looked where branches break
The glittering reaches of the flooded lake.

Another emblem there! That stormy white
But seems a concentration of the sky;
And, like the soul, it sails into the sight
And in the morning's gone, no man knows why;
And is so lovely that it sets to right
What knowledge or its lack had set awry,
So arrogantly pure, a child might think
It can be murdered with a spot of ink.

Sound of a stick upon the floor, a sound
From somebody that toils from chair to chair;
Beloved books that famous hands have bound,
Old marble heads, old pictures everywhere;
Great rooms where travelled men and children found
Content or joy; a last inheritor
Where none has reigned that lacked a name and fame
Or out of folly into folly came.

A spot whereon the founders lived and died
Seemed once more dear than life; ancestral trees,
Or gardens rich in memory glorified
Marriages, alliances and families
And every bride's ambition satisfied.
Where fashion or mere fantasy decrees
We shift about --- all that great glory spent ---
Like some poor Arab tribesman and his tent.

We were the last romantics – chose for theme
Traditional sanctity and loveliness;
Whatever's written in what poets name
The book of the people; whatever most can bless
The mind of man or elevate a rhyme;
But all is changed, that high horse riderless,
Though mounted in that saddle Homer rode
Where the swan drifts upon the darkening flood.

BYZANTIUM
1933

The unpurged images of day recede;
The Emperor's drunken soldiery are abed;
Night resonance recedes, night-walkers' song
After great cathedral gong;
A starlit or a moonlit dome disdains
All that man is,
All mere complexities,
The fury and the mire of human veins.

Before me floats an image, man or shade,
Shade more than man, more image than a shade;
For Hades' bobbin bound in mummy-cloth
May unwind the winding path;
A mouth that has no moisture and no breath
Breathless mouths may summon;
I hail the superhuman;
I call it death-in-life and life-in-death.

Miracle, bird or golden handiwork,
More miracle than bird or handiwork,
Planted on the star-lit golden bough,
Can like the cocks of Hades crow,
Or, by the moon embittered, scorn aloud
In glory of changeless metal
Common bird or petal
And all complexities of mire or blood.
At midnight on the Emperor's pavement flit
Flames that no faggot feeds, nor steel has lit,
Nor storm disturbs, flames begotten of flame,
Where blood-begotten spirits come
And all complexities of fury leave,
Dying into a dance,
An agony of trance,
An agony of flame that cannot singe a sleeve.

Astraddle on the dolphin's mire and blood,
Spirit after spirit! The smithies break the flood,
The golden smithies of the Emperor!
Marbles of the dancing floor
Break bitter furies of complexity,
Those images that yet
Fresh images beget,
That dolphin-torn, that gong-tormented sea.

CRAZY JANE AND THE BISHOP
1933

Bring me to the blasted oak
That I, midnight upon the stroke,
(All find safety in the tomb.)
May call down curses on his head
Because of my dear Jack that's dead.
Coxcomb was the least he said:
The solid man and the coxcomb.

Nor was he Bishop when his ban
Banished Jack the Journeyman
(All find safety in the tomb.)
Nor so much as parish priest,
Yet he, an old book in his fist,
Cried that we lived like beast and beast:
The solid man and the coxcomb.

The Bishop has a skin, God knows,
Wrinkled like the foot of a goose,
(All find safety in the tomb.)
Nor can he hide in holy black
The heron's hunch upon his back,
But a birch-tree stood my Jack:
The solid man and the coxcomb.

Jack had my virginity,
And bids me to the oak, for he
(All find safety in the tomb.)
Wanders out into the night
And there is shelter under it,
But should that other come, I spit:
The solid man and the coxcomb.

CRAZY JANE REPROVED
1933

I care not what the sailors say:
All those dreadful thunder-stones,
All that storm that blots the day
Can but show that Heaven yawns;
Great Europa played the fool
That changed the lover for a bull.
Fol de rol, fol de rol.

To round that shell's elaborate whorl,
Adorning every secret track
With the delicate mother-of-pearl,
Made the joints of Heaven crack:
So never hang your heart upon
A roaring, ranting journeyman.
Fol de rol, fol de rol.

CRAZY JANE ON THE DAY OF JUDGEMENT
1933

'Love is all
Unsatisfied
That cannot take the whole
Body and soul';
And that is what Jane said.

'Take the sour
If you take me,
I can scoff and lour
And scold for an hour.'
'That's certainly the case,' said he.

'Naked I lay,
The grass my bed;
Naked and hidden away,
That black day';
And that is what Jane said.

'What can be shown?
What true love be?
All could be known or shown
If Time were but gone.'
'That's certainly the case,' said he.

CRAZY JANE AND JACK THE JOURNEYMAN
1933

I know, although when looks meet
I tremble to the bone,
The more I leave the door unlatched
The sooner love is gone,
For love is but a skein unwound
Between the dark and dawn.

A lonely ghost the ghost is
That to God shall come;
I–love's skein upon the ground,
My body in the tomb–
Shall leap into the light lost
In my mother's womb.

But were I left to lie alone
In an empty bed,
The skein so bound us ghost to ghost
When he turned his head
Passing on the road that night,
Mine must walk when dead.

CRAZY JANE TALKS WITH THE BISHOP
1933

I met the Bishop on the road
And much said he and I.
'Those breasts are flat and fallen now,
Those veins must soon be dry;
Live in a heavenly mansion,
Not in some foul sty.'

'Fair and foul are near of kin,
And fair needs foul,' I cried.
'My friends are gone, but that's a truth
Nor grave nor bed denied,
Learned in bodily lowliness
And in the heart's pride.

'A woman can be proud and stiff
When on love intent;
But love has pitched his mansion in
The place of excrement;
For nothing can be sole or whole
That has not been rent.'

CRAZY JANE GROWN OLD LOOKS AT THE DANCERS
1933

I found that ivory image there
Dancing with her chosen youth,
But when he wound her coal-black hair
As tough to strangle her, no scream
Or bodily movement did I dare,
Eyes under eyelids did so gleam;
Love is like the lion's tooth.

When she, and though some said she played
I said that she had danced heart's truth,
Drew a knife to strike him dead,
I could but leave him to his fate;
For no matter what is said
They had all that had their hate;
Love is like the lion's tooth.

Did he die or did she die?
Seemed to die or died they both?
God be with the times when I
Cared not a thraneen for what chanced
So that I had the limbs to try
Such a dance as there was danced—
Love is like the lion's tooth.

GIRL'S SONG
1933

I went out alone
To sing a song or two,
My fancy on a man,
And you know who.

Another came in sight
That on a stick relied
To hold himself upright;
I sat and cried.

And that was all my song—
When everything is told,
Saw I an old man young
Or young man old?

YOUNG MAN'S SONG
1933

'She will change,' I cried,
'Into a withered crone.'
The heart in my side,
That so still had lain,
In noble rage replied
And beat upon the bone:

'Uplift those eyes and throw
Those glances unafraid:
She would as bravely show
Did all the fabric fade;
No withered crone I saw
Before the world was made.'

Abashed by that report,
For the heart cannot lie,
I knelt in the dirt.
And all shall bend the knee
To my offended heart
Until it pardon me.

AFTER LONG SILENCE
1933

Speech after long silence; it is right,
All other lovers being estranged or dead,
Unfriendly lamplight hid under its shade,
The curtains drawn upon unfriendly night,
That we descant and yet again descant
Upon the supreme theme of Art and Song:
Bodily decrepitude is wisdom; young
We loved each other and were ignorant.

MAD AS THE MIST AND SNOW
1933

Bolt and bar the shutter,
For the foul winds blow:
Our minds are at their best this night,
And I seem to know
That everything outside us is
Mad as the mist and snow.

Horace there by Homer stands,
Plato stands below,
And here is Tully's open page.
How many years ago
Were you and I unlettered lads
Mad as the mist and snow?

You ask what makes me sigh, old friend,
What makes me shudder so?
I shudder and I sigh to think
That even Cicero
And many-minded Homer were
Mad as the mist and snow.

THOSE DANCING DAYS ARE GONE
1933

Come, let me sing into your ear;
Those dancing days are gone,
All that silk and satin gear;
Crouch upon a stone,
Wrapping that foul body up
In as foul a rag:
I carry the sun in a golden cup,
The moon in a silver bag.

Curse as you may I sing it through;
What matter if the knave
That the most could pleasure you,
The children that he gave,
Are somewhere sleeping like a top
Under a marble flag?
I carry the sun in a golden cup,
The moon in a silver bag.

I thought it out this very day,
Noon upon the clock,
A man may put pretence away
Who leans upon a stick,
May sing, and sing until he drop,
Whether to maid or hag:
I carry the sun in a golden cup,
The moon in a silver bag.

'I AM OF IRELAND'
1933

'I am of Ireland,
And the Holy Land of Ireland,
And time runs on,' cried she.
'Come out of charity,
Come dance with me in Ireland.'

One man, one man alone
In that outlandish gear,
One solitary man
Of all that rambled there
Had turned his stately head.
'That is a long way off,
And time runs on,' he said,
'And the night grows rough.'

'I am of Ireland,
And the Holy Land of Ireland,
And time runs on,' cried she.
'Come out of charity,
Come dance with me in Ireland.'

'The fiddlers are all thumbs,
Or the fiddle-string accursed,
The drums and the kettledrums
And the trumpets all are burst,
And the trombone,' cried he,
'The trumpet and trombone,'
And cocked a malicious eye,
'But time runs on, runs on.'

'I am of Ireland,
And the Holy Land of Ireland,
And time runs on,' cried she.
'Come out of charity,
Come dance with me in Ireland.'

THE DELPHIC ORACLE UPON PLOTINUS
1933

Behold that great Plotinus swim,
Buffeted by such seas;
Bland Rhadamanthus beckons him,
But the Golden Race looks dim,
Salt blood blocks his eyes.

Scattered on the level grass
Or winding through the grove
Plato there and Minos pass,
There stately Pythagoras
And all the choir of Love.

A LAST CONFESSION
1933

What lively lad most pleasured me
Of all that with me lay?
I answer that I gave my soul
And loved in misery,
But had great pleasure with a lad
That I loved bodily.

Flinging from his arms I laughed
To think his passion such
He fancied that I gave a soul
Did but our bodies touch,
And laughed upon his breast to think
Beast gave beast as much.

I gave what other women gave
That stepped out of their clothes,
But when this soul, its body off,
Naked to naked goes,
He it has found shall find therein
What none other knows,

161

And give his own and take his own
And rule in his own right;
And though it loved in misery
Close and cling so tight,
There's not a bird of day that dare
Extinguish that delight.

ALTERNATIVE SONG FOR THE SEVERED HEAD IN
'THE KING OF THE GREAT CLOCK TOWER'
1934

Saddle and ride, I heard a man say,
Out of Ben Bulben and Knocknarea,
What says the Clock in the Great Clock Tower?
All those tragic characters ride
But turn from Rosses' crawling tide,
The meet's upon the mountain-side.
A slow low note and an iron bell.

What brought them there so far from their home,
Cuchulain that fought night long with the foam,
What says the Clock in the Great Clock Tower?
Niamh that rode on it; lad and lass
That sat so still and played at the chess?
What but heroic wantonness?
A slow low note and an iron bell.

Aleel, his Countess; Hanrahan
That seemed but a wild wenching man;
What says the Clock in the Great Clock Tower?
And all alone comes riding there
The King that could make his people stare,
Because he had feathers instead of hair.
A slow low note and an iron bell

LAPIS LAZULI
1938

I have heard that hysterical women say
They are sick of the palette and fiddle-bow,
Of poets that are always gay,
For everybody knows or else should know
That if nothing drastic is done
Aeroplane and Zeppelin will come out,
Pitch like King Billy bomb-balls in
Until the town lie beaten flat.

All perform their tragic play,
There struts Hamlet, there is Lear,
That's Ophelia, that Cordelia;
Yet they, should the last scene be there,
The great stage curtain about to drop,
If worthy their prominent part in the play,
Do not break up their lines to weep.
They know that Hamlet and Lear are gay;
Gaiety transfiguring all that dread.

All men have aimed at, found and lost;
Black out; Heaven blazing into the head:
Tragedy wrought to its uttermost.
Though Hamlet rambles and Lear rages,
And all the drop – scenes drop at once
Upon a hundred thousand stages,
It cannot grow by an inch or an ounce.

On their own feet they came, or on shipboard,
Camel-back, horse-back, ass-back, mule-back,
Old civilisations put to the sword.
Then they and their wisdom went to rack:
No handiwork of Callimachus,
Who handled marble as if it were bronze,
Made draperies that seemed to rise
When sea-wind swept the corner, stands;
His long lamp-chimney shaped like the stem
Of a slender palm, stood but a day;
All things fall and are built again,
And those that build them again are gay.

Two Chinamen, behind them a third,
Are carved in lapis lazuli,
Over them flies a long-legged bird,
A symbol of longevity;
The third, doubtless a serving man,
Carries a musical instrument.

Every discoloration of the stone,
Every accidental crack or dent,
Seems a water-course or an avalanche,
Or lofty slope where it still snows
Though doubtless plum or cherry-branch
Sweetens the little half-way house
Those Chinamen climb towards, and I
Delight to imagine them seated there;
There, on the mountain and the sky,
On all the tragic scene they stare.
One asks for mournful melodies;
Accomplished fingers begin to play.
Their eyes mid many wrinkles, their eyes,
Their ancient, glittering eyes, are gay.

THE THREE BUSHES
1938

Said lady once to lover,
'None can rely upon
A love that lacks its proper food;
And if your love were gone
How could you sing those songs of love?
I should be blamed, young man.
   O my dear, O my dear.

'Have no lit candles in your room,'
That lovely lady said,
'That I at midnight by the clock
May creep into your bed,
For if I saw myself creep in
I think I should drop dead.'
   O my dear, O my dear.

'I love a man in secret,
Dear chambermaid,' said she.
'I know that I must drop down dead
If he stop loving me,
Yet what could I but drop down dead
If I lost my chastity?
O my dear, O my dear.

'So you must lie beside him
And let him think me there.
And maybe we are all the same
Where no candles are,
And maybe we are all the same
That strip the body bare.'
O my dear, O my dear.

But no dogs barked, and midnights chimed,
And through the chime she'd say,
'That was a lucky thought of mine,
My lover looked so gay';
But heaved a sigh if the chambermaid
Looked half asleep all day.
O my dear, O my dear.

'No not another song,' said he,
'Because my lady came
A year ago for the first time
At midnight to my room,
And I must lie between the sheets
When the clock begins to chime.'
                    O my dear, O my dear.

'A laughing, crying, sacred song,
A leching song,' they said.
Did ever men hear such a song?
No, but that day they did.
Did ever man ride such a race?
No, no until he rode.
                    O my dear, O my dear.

But when his horse had put its hoof
Into a rabbit hole
He dropped upon his head and died.
His lady saw it all
And dropped and died thereon, for she
Loved him with her soul.
                    O my dear, O my dear.

The chambermaid lived long, and took
Their graves into her charge,
And there two bushes planted
That when they had grown large
Seemed sprung from but a single root
So did their roses merge.
O my dear, O my dear.

When she was old and dying,
The priest came where she was;
She made a full confession.
Long looked he in her face,
And O he was a good man
And understood her case.
O my dear, O my dear.

He bade them take and bury her
Beside her lady's man,
And set a rose tree on her grave,
And now none living can,
When they have plucked a rose there,
Know where its roots began.
O my dear, O my dear.

THE LADY'S FIRST SONG
1938

I turn round
Like a dumb beast in a show,
Neither know what I am
Nor where I go,
My language beaten
Into one name;
I am in love
And that is my shame.
What hurts the soul
My soul adores,
No better than a beast
Upon all fours.

THE LADY'S SECOND SONG
1938

What sort of man is coming
To lie between your feet?
What matter, we are but women.
Wash; make your body sweet;
I have cupboards of dried fragrance,
I can strew the sheet.
             The Lord have mercy upon us.

He shall love my soul as though
Body were not at all,
He shall love your body
Untroubled by the soul,
Love cram love's two divisions
Yet keep his substance whole.
             The Lord have mercy upon us.

Soul must learn a love that is
Proper to my breast,
Limbs a love in common
With every noble beast.
If soul may look and body touch,
Which is the more blest?
　　　　The Lord have mercy upon us.

THE LADY'S THIRD SONG
1938

When you and my true lover meet
And he plays tunes between your feet,
Speak no evil of the soul
Nor think that body is the whole,
For I that am is his daylight lady
Know worse evil of the body;
But in honour split his love
Till either neither have enough,
That I may hear if we should kiss
A contrapuntal serpent hiss,
You, should hand explore a thigh,
All the labouring heavens sigh.

THE LOVER'S SONG
1938

Bird sighs for the air,
Thought for I know not where,
For the womb the seed sighs.
Now sinks the same rest
On mind, on nest,
On straining thighs.

THE CHAMBERMAID'S FIRST SONG
1938

How came this ranger
Now sunk in rest,
Stranger with stranger,
On my cold breast?
What's left to sigh for?
Strange night has come;
God's love has hidden him
Out of all harm,
Pleasure has made him
Weak as a worm.

THE CHAMBERMAID'S SECOND SONG
1938

From pleasure of the bed,
Dull as a worm,
His rod and its butting head
Limp as a worm,
His spirit that has fled
Blind as a worm.

A Crazed Girl
1938

That crazed girl improvising her music,
Her poetry, dancing upon the shore,
Her soul in division from itself
Climbing, falling she knew not where,
Hiding amid the cargo of a steamship,
Her knee-cap broken, that girl I declare
A beautiful lofty thing, or a thing
Heroically lost, heroically found.

No matter what disaster occurred
She stood in desperate music wound,
Wound, wound, and she made in her triumph
Where the bales and the baskets lay
No common intelligible sound
But sang, 'O sea-starved, hungry sea.'

ROGER CASEMENT
1938

I say that Roger Casement
Did what he had to do.
He died upon the gallows,
But that is nothing new.

Afraid they might be beaten
Before the bench of Time,
They turned a trick by forgery
And blackened his good name.

A perjurer stood ready
To prove their forgery true;
They gave it out to all the world,
And that is something new;

For Spring Rice had to whisper it,
Being their Ambassador,
And then the speakers got it
And writers by the score.

Come Tom and Dick, come all the troop
That cried it far and wide,
Come from the forger and his desk,
Desert the perjurer's side;

Come speak your bit in public
That some amends be made
To this most gallant gentleman
That is in quicklime laid.

THE WILD OLD WICKED MAN
1938

'Because I am mad about women
I am mad about the hills,'
Said that wild old wicked man
Who travels where God wills.
'Not to die on the straw at home,
Those hands to close these eyes,
That is all I ask, my dear,
From the old man in the skies.
                    Daybreak and a candle-end.

'Kind are all your words, my dear,
Do not the rest withhold.
Who can know the year, my dear,
When an old man's blood grows cold?
I have what no young man can have
Because he loves too much.
Words I have that can pierce the heart,
But what can he do but touch?'
                    Daybreak and a candle-end.

Then said she to that wild old man,
His stout stick under his hand,
'Love to give or to withhold
Is not at my command.
I gave it all to an older man:
That old man in the skies.
Hands that are busy with His beads
Can never close those eyes
    Daybreak and a candle-end.

'Go your ways, O go your ways,
I choose another mark,
Girls down on the seashore
Who understand the dark;
Bawdy talk for the fishermen;
A dance for the fisher-lads;
When dark hangs upon the water
They turn down their beds.
    Daybreak and a candle-end.

'A young man in the dark am I,
But a wild old man in the light,
That can make a cat laugh, or
Can touch by mother wit
Things hid in their marrow-bones
From time long passed away,
Hid from all those warty lads
That by their bodies lay.
    Daybreak and a candle-end.

'All men live in suffering,
I know as few can know,
Whether they take the upper road
Or stay content on the low,
Rower bent in his row-boat
Or weaver bent at his loom,
Horseman erect upon horseback
Or child hid in the womb.
                    Daybreak and a candle-end.

'That some stream of lightening
From the old man in the skies
Can burn out that suffering
No right-taught man denies.
But a coarse old man am I,
I choose the second best,
I forget it all awhile
Upon a woman's breast.'
                    Daybreak and a candle-end.

THE SPUR
1938

You think it horrible that lust and rage
Should dance attention upon my old age;
They were not such a plague when I was young;
What else have I to spur me into song?

THE MUNICIPAL GALLERY REVISITED
1938

I

Around me the images of thirty years:
An ambush; pilgrims at the water-side;
Casement upon trial, half hidden by the bars,
Guarded; Griffith staring in hysterical pride;
Kevin O'Higgins' countenance that wears
A gentle questioning look that cannot hide
A soul incapable of remorse or rest;
A revolutionary soldier kneeling to be blessed;

II

An Abbot or Archbishop with an upraised hand
Blessing the Tricolour. 'This is not,' I say,
'The dead Ireland of my youth, but an Ireland
The poets have imagined, terrible and gay.'

Before a woman's portrait suddenly I stand,
Beautiful and gentle in her Venetian way.
I met her all but fifty years ago
For twenty minutes in some studio.

III

Heart-smitten with emotion I sink down,
My heart recovering with covered eyes;
Wherever I had looked I had looked upon
My permanent or impermanent images:
Augusta Gregory's son; her sister's son,
Hugh Lane, 'onlie begetter' of all these;
Hazel Lavery living and dying, that tale
As though some ballad-singer had sung it all;

IV

Mancini's portrait of Augusta Gregory,
'Greatest since Rembrandt,' according to John Synge;
A great ebullient portrait certainly;
But where is the brush that could show anything
Of all that pride and that humility?
And I am in despair that time may bring
Approved patterns of women or of men
But not that selfsame excellence again.

V

My mediaeval knees lack health until they bend,
But in that woman, in that household where
Honour had lived so long, all lacking found.
Childless I thought, 'My children may find here
Deep-rooted things, ' but never foresaw its end,
And now that end has come I have not wept;
No fox can foul the lair the badger swept –

VI

(An image out of Spenser and the common tongue).
John Synge, I and Augusta Gregory, thought
All that we did, all that we said or sang
Must come from contact with the soil, from that
Contact everything Antaeus-like grew strong.
We three alone in modern times had brought
Everything down to that sole test again,
Dream of the noble and the beggar-man.

VII

And here's John Synge himself, that rooted man,
'Forgetting human words,' a grave deep face.
You that would judge me, do not judge alone
This book or that, come to this hallowed place
Where my friends' portraits hang and look thereon;
Ireland's history in their lineaments trace;
Think where man's glory most begins and ends,
And say my glory was I had such friends.

News for the Delphic Oracle
1939

I

There all the golden codgers lay,
There the silver dew,
And the great water sighed for love,
And the wind sighed too.
Man-picker Niamh leant and sighed
By Oisin on the grass;
There sighed amid his choir of love
Tall Pythagoras.
Plotinus came and looked about,
The salt-flakes on his breast,
And having stretched and yawned awhile
Lay sighing like the rest.

II

Straddling each a dolphin's back
And steadied by a fin,
Those Innocents re-live their death,
Their wounds open again.
The ecstatic waters laugh because
Their cries are sweet and strange,
Through their ancestral patterns dance,
And the brute dolphins plunge
Until, in some cliff-sheltered bay
Where wades the choir of love
Proffering its sacred laurel crowns,
They pitch their burdens off.

III

Slim adolescence that a nymph has stripped,
Peleus on Thetis stares.
Her limbs are delicate as an eyelid,
Love has blinded him with tears;
But Thetis' belly listens.
Down the mountain walls
From where Pan's cavern is
Intolerable music falls.
Foul goat-head, brutal arm appear,
Belly, shoulder, bum,
Flash fishlike; nymphs and satyrs
Copulate in the foam.

LONG-LEGGED FLY
1939

That civilisation may not sink,
Its great battle lost,
Quiet the dog, tether the pony
To a distant post;
Our master Caesar is in the tent
Where the maps are spread,
His eyes fixed upon nothing,
A hand under his head.
Like a long-legged fly upon the stream
His mind moves upon silence.

That the topless towers be burnt
And men recall that face,
Move gently if move you must
In this lonely place.
She thinks, part woman, three parts a child,
That nobody looks; her feet
Practise a tinker shuffle
Picked up on a street.

Like a long-legged fly upon the stream
Her mind moves upon silence.

That girls at puberty may find
The first Adam in their thought,
Shut the door of the Pope's chapel,
Keep those children out.
There on that scaffolding reclines
Michael Angelo.
With no more sound than the mice make
His hand moves to and fro.
Like a long-legged fly upon the stream
His mind moves upon silence.

WHY SHOULD NOT OLD MEN BE MAD?
1939

Why should not old men be mad?
Some have known a likely lad
That had a sound fly-fisher's wrist
Turn to a drunken journalist;
A girl that knew all Dante once
Live to bear children to a dunce;
A Helen of social welfare dream,
Climb on a wagonette to scream.
Some think it a matter of course that chance
Should starve good men and bad advance,
That if their neighbours figured plain,
As though upon a lighted screen,
No single story would they find
Of an unbroken happy mind,
A finish worthy of the start.
Young men know nothing of this sort,
Observant old men know it well;
And when they know what old books tell,
And that no better can be had,
Know why an old man should be mad.

CRAZY JANE ON THE MOUNTAIN
1939

I am tired of cursing the Bishop,
(Said Crazy Jane)
Nine books or nine hats
Would not make him a man.
I have found something worse
To meditate on.
A King had some beautiful cousins,
But where are they gone?
Battered to death in a cellar,
And he stuck to his throne.
Last night I lay on the mountain,
(Said Crazy Jane)
There in a two-horsed carriage
That on two wheels ran
Great-bladdered Emer sat,
Her violent man
Cuchulain sat at her side;
Thereupon,
Propped upon my two knees,
I kissed a stone;
I lay stretched out in the dirt
And I cried tears down.

THE CIRCUS ANIMALS' DESERTION
1939

I

I sought a theme and sought for it in vain,
I sought it daily for six weeks or so.
Maybe at last, being but a broken man,
I must be satisfied with my heart, although
Winter and summer till old age began
My circus animals were all on show,
Those stilted boys, that burnished chariot,
Lion and woman and the Lord knows what.

II

What can I but enumerate old themes?
First that sea-rider Oisin led by the nose
Through three enchanted islands, allegorical dreams,
Vain gaiety, vain battle, vain repose,

Themes of the embittered heart, or so it seems,
That might adorn old songs or courtly shows;
But what cared I that set him on to ride,
I, starved for the bosom of his faery bride?

And then a counter-truth filled out its play,
The Countess Cathleen was the name I gave it;
She, pity-crazed, had given her soul away,
But masterful Heaven had intervened to save it.
I thought my dear must her own soul destroy,
So did fanaticism and hate enslave it,
And this brought forth a dream and soon enough
This dream itself had all my thought and love.

And when the Fool and Blind Man stole the bread
Cuchulain fought the ungovernable sea;
Heart-mysteries there, and yet when all is said
It was the dream itself enchanted me:
Character isolated by a deed
To engross the present and dominate memory.
Players and painted stage took all my love,
And not those things that they were emblems of.

III

Those masterful images because complete
Grew in pure mind, but out of what began?
A mound of refuse or the sweepings of a street,
Old kettles, old bottles, and a broken can,
Old iron, old bones, old rags, that raving slut
Who keeps the till. Now that my ladder's gone,
I must lie down where all the ladders start,
In the foul rag-and-bone shop of the heart.

CUCHULAIN COMFORTED
1939

A man that had six mortal wounds, a man
Violent and famous, strode among the dead;
Eyes stared out of the branches and were gone.

Then certain Shrouds that muttered head to head
Came and were gone. He leant upon a tree
As though to meditate on wounds and blood.

A Shroud that seemed to have authority
Among those bird-like things came, and let fall
A bundle of linen. Shrouds by two and three

Came creeping up because the man was still.
And thereupon that linen-carrier said:
'Your life can grow much sweeter if you will

'Obey our ancient rule and make a shroud;
Mainly because of what we only know
The rattle of those arms makes us afraid.

'We thread the needles' eyes, and all we do
All must together do.' That done, the man
Took up the nearest and began to sew.

'Now must we sing and sing the best we can,
But first you must be told our character:
Convicted cowards all, by kindred slain

'Or driven from home and left to die in fear.'
They sang, but had nor human tunes nor words,
Though all was done in common as before;

They had changed their throats and had the throats of
    birds.

UNDER BEN BULBEN
1939

I

Swear by what the sages spoke
Round the Mareotic Lake
That the Witch of Atlas knew,
Spoke and set the cocks a-crow.

Swear by those horsemen, by those women
Complexion and form prove superhuman,
That pale, long-visaged company
That air in immortality
Completeness of their passions won;
Now they ride the wintry dawn
Where Ben Bulben sets the scene.

Here's the gist of what they mean.

II

Many times man lives and dies
Between his two eternities,
That of race and that of soul,
And ancient Ireland knew it all.
Whether man die in his bed
Or the rifle knock him dead,
A brief parting from those dear
Is the worst man has to fear.
Though grave-diggers' toil is long,
Sharp their spades, their muscles strong,
They but thrust their buried men
Back in the human mind again.

III

You that Mitchel's prayer have heard,
'Send war in our time, O Lord!'
Know that when all words are said
And a man is fighting mad,
Something drops from eyes long blind,
He completes his partial mind,
For an instant stands at ease,
Laughs aloud, his heart at peace.
Even the wisest man grows tense
With some sort of violence

Before he can accomplish fate,
Know his work or choose his mate.

IV

Poet and sculptor, do the work,
Nor let the modish painter shirk
What his great forefathers did,
Bring the soul of man to God,
Make him fill the cradles right.

Measurement began our might:
Forms a stark Egyptian thought,
Forms that gentler Phidias wrought.
Michael Angelo left a proof
On the Sistine Chapel roof,
Where but half-awakened Adam
Can disturb globe-trotting Madam
Till her bowels are in heat,
Proof that there's a purpose set
Before the secret working mind:
Profane perfection of mankind.

Quattrocento put in paint
On backgrounds for a God or Saint
Gardens where a soul's at ease;
Where everything that meets the eye,

Flowers and grass and cloudless sky,
Resemble forms that are or seem
When sleepers wake and yet still dream,
And when it's vanished still declare,
With only bed and bedstead there,
That heavens had opened.
                        Gyres run on;
When that greater dream had gone
Calvert and Wilson, Blake and Claude,
Prepared a rest for the people of God,
Palmer's phrase, but after that
Confusion fell upon our thought.

V

Irish poets, learn your trade,
Sing whatever is well made,
Scorn the sort now growing up
All out of shape from toe to top,
Their unremembering hearts and heads
Base-born products of base beds.
Sing the peasantry, and then
Hard-riding country gentlemen,
The holiness of monks, and after
Porter-drinkers' randy laughter;
Sing the lords and ladies gay
That were beaten into the clay

Through seven heroic centuries;
Cast your mind on other days
That we in coming days may be
Still the indomitable Irishry.

VI

Under bare Ben Bulben's head
In Drumcliff churchyard Yeats is laid.
An ancestor was rector there
Long years ago, a church stands near,
By the road an ancient cross.
No marble, no conventional phrase;
On limestone quarried near the spot
By his command these words are cut:

> *Cast a cold eye*
> *On life, on death.*
> *Horseman, pass by!*

PLAYS

THE COUNTESS CATHLEEN
1892

Cathleen. Bend down your faces, Oona and Aleel;
I gaze upon them as the swallow gazes
Upon the nest under the eave, before
She wander the loud waters. Do not weep
Too great a while, for there is many a candle
On the High Altar though one fall. Aleel,
Who sang about the dancers of the woods
That know not the hard burden of the world,
Having but breath in their kind bodies, farewell!
And farewell, Oona, you who played with me,
And bore me in your arms about the house
When I was but a child and therefore happy,
Therefore happy, even like those that dance.
The storm is in my hair and I must go. [Scene V]

Oona. Tell them who walk upon the floor of peace
That I would die and go to her I love;
The years like great black oxen tread the world,
And God the herdsman goads them on behind,
And I am broken by their passing feet. [Scene V]

THE LAND OF HEART'S DESIRE
1894

The wind blows out of the gates of the day,
The wind blows over the lonely of heart,
And the lonely of heart is withered away;
(While the faeries dance in a place apart,
Shaking their milk-white feet in a ring,
Tossing their mil-white arms in the air;
For they hear the wind laugh and murmur and sing
Of a land where even the old are fair,
And even the wise are merry of tongue;
But I heard a reed of Coolaney say –
'When the wind has laughed and murmured and sung,
The lonely of heart is withered away.')

CATHLEEN NI HOULIHAN
1902

Peter [to Patrick, laying a hand on his arm].
Did you see an old woman going down the path?

Patrick.
I did not, but I saw a young girl, and she had the
walk of a queen.

THE KING'S THRESHOLD
1904

Seanchan.
The four rivers that run there,
Through well-mown level ground,
Have come out of a blessed well
That is all bound and wound
By the great roots of an apple
And all the fowls of the air
Have gathered in the wide branches
And keep singing there.

THE SHADOWY WATERS
1911

Forgael. I cannot answer.
I can see nothing plain; all's mystery.
Yet sometimes there's a torch inside my head
That makes all clear, but when the light is gone
I have but images, analogies,
The mystic bread, the sacramental wine,
The red rose where the two shafts of the cross,
Body and soul, waking and sleep, death, life,
Whatever meaning ancient allegorists
Have settled on, are mixed into one joy.
For what's the rose but that? miraculous cries,
Old stories about mystic marriages,
Impossible truths? But when the torch is lit
All that is impossible is certain,
I plunge in the abyss.

DEIRDRE
1907

Love is an immoderate thing
And can never be content
Till it dip an ageing wing
Where some laughing element
Leaps and Time's old lanthorn dims.
What's the merit in love-play,
In the tumult of the limbs
That dies out before 'tis day,
Heart on heart, or mouth on mouth,
All that mingling of our breath,
When love-longing is but drouth
For the things come after death?

AT THE HAWK'S WELL
1917

[Songs for the unfolding and folding of the cloth]

Come to me, human faces,
Familiar memories;
I have found hateful eyes
Among the desolate places,
Unfaltering, unmoistened eyes.

Folly alone l cherish,
I choose it for my share;
Being but a mouthful of air,
I am content to perish;
I am but a mouthful of sweet air.

O lamentable shadows,
Obscurity of strife!
I choose a pleasant life
Among indolent meadows;
Wisdom must live a bitter life.

[They then fold up the cloth, singing.

'The man that I praise',
Cries out the empty well,
'Lives all his days
Where a hand on the bell
Can call the milch cows
To the comfortable door of his house.
Who but an idiot would praise
Dry stones in a well?'

'The man that I praise',
Cries out the leafless tree,
'Has married and stays
By an old hearth, and he
On naught has set store
But children and dogs on the floor.
Who but an idiot would praise
A withered tree?'

ON BAILE'S STRAND
1904

Cuchulain.
It's well that we should speak our minds out plainly,
For when we die we shall be spoken of
In many countries. We in our young days
Have seen the heavens like a burning cloud
Brooding upon the world, and being more
Than men can be now that cloud's lifted up,
We should be the more truthful. Conchubar,
I do not like your children – they have no pith,
No marrow in their bones, and will lie soft
Where you and I lie hard.

Conchubar.
You rail at them
Because you have no children of your own.

Cuchulain.
I think myself most lucky that I leave
No pallid ghost or mockery of a man

To drift and mutter in the corridors
Where I have laughed and sung.

Cuchulain.
I will give you gifts
That Aoife'll know, and all her people know,
To have come from me.   *[Showing cloak.*

My father gave me this.
He came to try me, rising up at dawn
Out of the cold dark of the rich sea.
He challenged me to battle, but before
My sword had touched his sword, told me his name,
Gave me this cloak, and vanished. It was woven
By women of the Country-under-Wave
Out of the fleeces of the sea. O! tell her
I was afraid, or tell her what you will.
No; tell her that I heard a raven croak
On the north side of the house, and was afraid.

First Woman.
Life drifts between a fool and a blind man
To the end, and nobody can know his end.

THE DREAMING OF THE BONES
1919

[Song for the folding and unfolding of the cloth]

Why does my heart beat so?
Did not a shadow pass?
It passed but a moment ago.
Who can have trod in the grass?
What rogue is night-wandering?
Have not old writers said
That dizzy dreams can spring
From the dry bones of the dead?
And many a night it seems
That all the valley fills
With those fantastic dreams.
They overflow the hills,
So passionate is a shade,
Like wine that fills to the top
A grey-green cup of jade,
Or maybe an agate cup.

I

At the grey round of the hill
Music of a lost kingdom
Runs, runs and is suddenly still.
The winds out of Clare-Galway
Carry it: suddenly it is still.

I have heard in the night air
A wandering airy music;
And moidered in that snare
A man is lost of a sudden,
In that sweet wandering snare.

What finger first began
Music of a lost kingdom?
They dream that laughed in the sun.
Dry bones that dream are bitter,
They dream and darken our sun.

Those crazy fingers play
A wandering airy music;
Our luck is withered away,
And wheat in the wheat-ear withered,
And the wind blows it away.

II

My heart ran wild when it heard
The curlew cry before dawn
And the eddying cat-headed bird;
But now the night is gone.
I have heard from far below
The strong March birds a-crow.
Stretch neck and clap the wing,
Red cocks, and crow!

CALVARY
1920

[Song for the folding and unfolding of the cloth]

First musician.
Lonely the sea-bird lies at her rest,
Blown like a dawn-blenched parcel of spray
Upon the wind, or follows her prey
Under a great wave's hollowing crest.

Second Musician.
God has not appeared to the birds.

Third Musician.
The ger-eagle has chosen his part
In blue-deep of the upper air
Where one-eyed day can meet his stare;
He is content with his savage heart.

Second Musician.
God has not appeared to the birds.

First Musician.
But where have last year's cygnets gone?
The lake is empty; why do they fling
White wing out beside white wing?
What can a swan need but a swan?

Second Musician.
God has not appeared to the birds.

A FULL MOON IN MARCH
1935

Second Attendant.
Every loutish lad in love
Thinks his wisdom great enough,
What cares love for this and that?
To make all his parish stare,
As though Pythagoras wandered there.
Crown of gold or dung of swine.

Should old Pythagoras fall in love
Little may he boast thereof.
What cares love for this and that?
Days go by in foolishness.
O how great their sweetness is!
Crown of gold or dung of swine.

Open wide those gleaming eyes,
That can make the loutish wise.
What cares love for this and that?
Make a leader of the schools

Thank the Lord all men are fools.
Crown of gold or dung of swine.

First Attendant
He has famished in a wilderness,
Braved lions for my sake,
And all men lie that say that I
Bade that swordsman take
His head from off his body
And set it on a stake.

He swore to sing my beauty
Though death itself forbade.
They lie that say, in mockery
Of all that lovers said,
Or in mere woman's cruelty
I bade them fetch his head.

O what innkeeper's daughter
Shared the Byzantine crown?
Girls that have governed cities,
Or burned great cities down,
Have bedded with their fancy-man
Whether king or clown;

Gave their bodies, emptied purses
For praise of clown or king,
Gave all the love that women know!

O they had their fling,
But never stood before a stake
And heard the dead lips sing.

                [Singing as Queen]
Child and darling, hear my song,
Never cry I did you wrong
Cry that wrong came not from me
But my virgin cruelty.
Great my love before you came,
Greater when I loved in shame,
Greatest when there broke from me
Storm of virgin cruelty.

Second Attendant [singing as Head].
I sing a song of Jack and Jill.
Jill had murdered Jack;
The moon shone brightly;
Ran up the hill, and round the hill,
Round the hill and back.
A full moon in March.
Jack had a hollow heart, for Jill
Had hung his heart on high;
The moon shone brightly;
Had hung his heart beyond the hill,
A-twinkle in the sky.
A full moon in March.

THE DEATH OF CUCHULAIN
1939

Singer.
The harlot sang to the beggar-man.
I meet them face to face,
Conall, Cuchulain, Usna's boys,
All that most ancient race;
Maeve had three in an hour, they say.
I adore those clever eyes,
Those muscular bodies, but can get
No grip upon their thighs.
I meet those long pale faces,
Hear their great horses, then
Recall what centuries have passed
Since they were living men.
That there are still some living
That do my limbs unclothe,
But that the flesh my flesh has gripped
I both adore and loathe.

Are those things that men adore and loathe
Their sole reality?
What stood in the Post Office
With Pearse and Connolly?
What comes out of the mountain
Where men first shed their blood?
Who thought Cuchulain till it seemed
He stood where they had stood?

No body like his body
Has modern woman borne,
But an old man looking back on life
Imagines it in scorn.
A statue's there to mark the place,
By Oliver Sheppard done.
So ends the tale that the harlot
Sang to the beggar-man.

PROSE
AND
SPEECHES

Behind Ireland fierce and militant, is Ireland poetic, passionate, remembering, idyllic, fanciful, and always patriotic.

[In Leisure Hour, 1889, 'Popular Ballad Poetry of Ireland']

When we remember the majesty of Cuchullin and the beauty of sorrowing Deirdre we should not forget that it is that majesty and that beauty which are immortal, and not the perishing tongue that first told of them.

[United Ireland, 1892]

All folk literature, and all literature that keeps the folk tradition, delights in unbounded and immortal things.

['The Celtic Element in Literature' (1902)]

The chief use I can be ... will be by introducing you to some other writers ... one always learns one's business from one's fellow workers.

[Letter to James Joyce, in Richard Ellman, James Joyce]

We have no longer in any country a literature as great as the literature of the old world, and that is because the newspapers, all kinds of second-rate books, the preoccupation of men with all kinds of practical changes, have driven the living imagination out of this world.

[In Samhain, 1904, 'First Principles']

'In dreams begins responsibility.'

[In Responsibilities (1914), Epigraph]

We make out of the quarrel with others, rhetoric, but of the quarrel with ourselves, poetry.

[Per Amica Silentia Lunae (1917), 'Anima Hominis', V]

The poet finds and makes his mask in disappointment, the hero in defeat.

[Per Amica Silentia Lunae (1917), 'Anima Hominis', IX]

[On his Nobel Prize medal]
It shows a young man listening to a Muse, who stands young and beautiful with a great lyre in her hand, and I think as I examine it, 'I was good looking once like that young man, but my unpracticed

verse was full of infirmity, my Muse old as it were;
and now I am old and rheumatic, and nothing to
look at, but my Muse is young.'

[The Bounty of Sweden (1925), 7]

A civilisation is a struggle to keep self-control.

[A Vision (1925), 'Dove or Swan']

It seems to me that true love is a discipline, and it
needs so much wisdom that the love of Solomon
and Sheba must have lasted, for all the silence of the
Scriptures.

[Estrangement: Being some fifty Thoughts from a
Diary kept in the year nineteen hundred and nine
(1926), 7]

I think that all happiness depends upon the energy to assume the mask of some other self; that all joyous or creative life is a rebirth as something not oneself, something which has no memory and is created in a moment and perpetually renewed.

[The Death of Synge and other Passages from an Old Diary (1928), 6]

A good writer should be so simple that he has no faults, only sins.

[The Death of Synge and other Passages from an Old Diary (1928), 41]

[On George Moore]
He had gone to Paris straight from his father's racing stables, from a house where there was no culture, as Symons and I understood that word, acquired copious inaccurate French, sat among art

235

students, young writers about to become famous, in some café; a man carved out of a turnip, looking out of astonished eyes.

[Dramatis Personae (1935), 7]

[On George Moore as a plagiarist]
'The man I object to,' said Moore, 'is the man who plagiarizes without knowing it; I always know; I took ten pages.' To Lady Gregory he said, 'We both quote well, but you always put inverted commas, I never do.'

[Dramatis Personae (1935), 20]

[Referring to Wilfred Owen]
He is all blood, dirt and sucked sugar stick ... There is every excuse for him but none for those who like him.

[In D. Wellesley (ed.), Letters on Poetry from W.B. Yeats to Dorothy Wellesley (1940), Letter, 21 December 1936]

I once boasted, copying the phrase from a letter of my father's, that I would write a poem 'cold and passionate as the dawn'.

[Essays and Introductions (1961), 'A General Introduction for my Work' (1937), 3]

The Irish mind has still, in country rapscallion or in Bernard Shaw, an ancient, cold, explosive, detonating impartiality. The English mind, excited by its newspaper proprietors and its schoolmasters, has turned into a bed-hot harlot.

[On the Boiler (1939), 'Ireland after the Revolution', III]

[An imaginary letter, 1931, to a schoolmaster]
My son is now between 9 and 10 and should begin Greek at once ... Do not teach him one word of Latin. The Roman people were the classic decadence, their literature form without matter. They destroyed Milton, the French seventeenth and our eighteenth century ...

[In J. Hone, W.B. Yeats 1865—1939 (1943), 18, 7]

When I think of all the books I have read, and of the wise words I have heard spoken, and of the anxiety I have given to parents and grandparents, and of the hopes that I have had, all life weighed in the scales of my own life seems to me preparation for something that never happens.

[Autobiographies (1955)]

[Of George Eliot]
She is magnificently ugly — deliciously hideous ...
now in this vast ugliness resides a most powerful
beauty which, in a very few minutes steals forth
and charms the mind.

[Attr.]

We against whom you have done this thing are no
petty people. We are one of the great stocks of
Europe. We are the people of Burke; we are the people of Grattan; we are the people of Swift, the people of Emmet, the people of Parnell. We have created the most of the modern literature of this country.
We have created the best of its political intelligence.

[Senate Speech, 1925]

[In conversation with John Sparrow, 1931]
The tragedy of sexual intercourse is the perpetual virginity of the soul.

[Attr. in A. Norman Jeffares, W.B. Yeats: man and poet (1949), 10 (i)]

[On being told how great an honour it was for self and country to win the Nobel Prize]
How much is it, Smyllie, how much is it?

[Attr. in W.R. Rodgers (ed.), Irish Literary Portraits (1972)]

[Speaking to playwright, Denis Johnston]
It's not a writer's business to hold opinions.

[The Guardian, 1977]

O'Connor: How are you?
W.B.Y.: Not very well, I can only write prose today.

INDEX TO TITLES
OF POEMS

INDEX TO FIRST LINES
OF POEMS

COLLINS CLASSICS

Complete Novels of Jane Austen
With introductions by Patrick O'Brian, Reginald Hill and others

Complete Novels of Anne Brontë
With introduction by Charlotte Cory

Complete Novels of Charlotte & Emily Brontë
With introductions by Hilary Mantel, Robert Barnard and others

Complete Works of Shakespeare
With introductions by Germaine Greer, Anthony Burgess and others

Complete Works of Oscar Wilde
With introductions by Vyvyan Holland, Merlin Holland and others

Complete Sherlock Holmes & Other Detective Stories by Sir Arthur Conan Doyle
With introduction by Owen Dudley Edwards

Complete Novels of Thomas Hardy
With introduction by Roy Hattersley

Five Classic Adventure Novels
With introduction by George MacDonald Fraser

COLLINS GEM

Bestselling Collins Gem titles include: